BORING MEETINGS

SUCK

GET MORE OUT OF YOUR MEETINGS, OR GET OUT OF MORE MEETINGS

JON PETZ

WILEY

John Wiley & Sons, Inc.

Published by John Wiley & Sons, Inc., Hoboken, New Jersey.
Published simultaneously in Canada.

For general information on our other products and services or for technical support, please contact our Customer Care Department within the United States at (800) 762-2974, outside the United States at (317) 572-3993 or fax (317) 572-4002.

Wiley also publishes its books in a variety of electronic formats. Some content that appears in print may not be available in electronic books. For more information about Wiley products, visit our web site at www.wiley.com.

Library of Congress Cataloging-in-Publication Data:

Petz, Jon.
  Boring meetings suck: get more out of your meetings, or get out of more meetings / Jon Petz.
    p. cm.
  Includes index.
  ISBN 978-1-118-00462-3 (cloth)
  ISBN 978-1-118-04382-0 (ebk)
  ISBN 978-1-118-04383-7 (ebk)
  ISBN 978-1-118-04384-4 (ebk)
  1. Business meetings. I. Title.
  HF5734.5.P475 2011
  658.4'56—dc22

                                                                    2010049550

Printed in the United States of America

10 9 8 7 6 5 4 3

Boring Meetings Suck *is dedicated*
to the ladies who allow
my wonderful life to have meaning
and not suck: Stacey, Sydney,
Mackenzie, and Madison.

It is also dedicated to all those
like-minded souls who have ever been
in meetings that were a colossal waste
of time, energy, creativity, and money
and are willing to do something about it.

I further dedicate this to three special people
who have made a tremendous impact on
my personal and professional life in ways
greater than they ever will realize.
Thank you, Larry and Cindy H., and Jeffrey D.

Contents

Agenda Item 4

Why Everyday Office Meetings Suck . . . Skip This and You're Screwed   49

Agenda Item 5

Your Presentation Sucks . . . Really, *Yours* Sucks   93

Contents

Contents

Foreword

What's that loud sucking sound?

Oh . . . it's your MEETING.

You'd think you'd know by now.

Meetings suck.

And BORING meetings?

They suck the most.

When Jon Petz and I began collaborating on the original version of this book in 2006, we decided to poke fun at some of the worst meetings we'd ever had the misfortune to attend. We offered humorous suggestions on how to improve a bad situation—all the boring meetings you have to facilitate *and* attend.

But you weren't *listening*.

You went right on having your boring meetings, inviting even more attendees and putting them into a coma with your pointless PowerPoint slides.

What choice did Jon have?

You've forced him to create a bigger, badder, louder alarm clock to wake you up to all the time, energy, creativity, and money you're wasting by meeting in boring and banal ways.

Consider this revised and updated version of *Boring Meetings Suck* a paginated intervention—a tough-love text to help you help yourself. Jon has added chapters about using technology to reduce the number of meetings, identifying meeting types, and helping you to decide whether a meeting is even necessary in the first place. (That's right. Nobody said you *had* to hold meetings at all!)

But take it slow.

The information is this book flies in the face of how the corporate world has trained you. At first, use the *Boring Meetings Sucks* SRDs (Suckification Reduction Devices) to lower the suck level of your meetings. Once you're comfortable doing that, then strive to eliminate that sucking sound altogether.

I suggest you give this book to your boss (personally or anonymously), hand it to anyone in charge of a committee, or conveniently leave it in plain sight on the conference room table. Most important, keep your own copy close by and follow the advice within. You'll see how it can benefit meeting *attendees* just as much as meeting *facilitators*! Yes, even as an attendee, you can use these tips to suggest meeting alternatives when possible and speed up the meetings you can't avoid altogether.

So then what's that loud sucking sound?

Must be someone else's meeting . . .

—Don The Idea Guy Snyder
www.dontheideaguy.com

Agenda Item 1

Boring Meetings Suck . . . so Why Do We Have 'Em?

Why do so many meetings have to suck . . .

So badly?
So consistently?

How many millions upon millions of people are wondering every day: *Why* am I stuck in this meeting? I have far better things to do than listen to people put in their two cents several times over. And how on earth do I get out of here?

They're also asking—

- Why was I even invited?

- Why is this presenter *reading* PowerPoint slides? Couldn't this person have just mailed the presentation to everyone and skipped the meeting?

- Why is this meeting going a full hour even though we finished the agenda in 35 minutes?

- Why is this conference call being constantly interrupted with the question, "Who just joined?"

- Why is this meeting wasting thousands of dollars of human capital by endlessly talking about problems but never solving them?

1

- Why is the boss holding a meeting to get our input, but all the while wearing the intended solution on his or her sleeve?

- Why is the dreaded annual meeting a time we're told what we're doing wrong and preached to all day? Don't they ever want to hear from us?

Ever felt like this? *Then you're in the right spot!*

Where did we, as humans, go wrong? I think it goes all the way back to Adam meeting Eve. The objective of their meeting—to stay away from that fruit—was never clearly identified as an action item. And not much has changed since then.

In September 2010, a front-page story in *USA Today* reported that 49 percent of all office meetings are found to be "wasted time."* Given that, let me be perfectly clear: **Meetings aren't the problem. The people running them are!**

Humankind has landed on the moon, embraced new technologies at breakneck speed, and advanced in so many ways, but we are still plagued with this billion-dollar problem of running meetings poorly! No one has stood up to aggressively battle this plague! Something needs to change in a way that will be received, understood, and implemented by the everyday worker.

It's going to take a revolution, folks! Workers of the world, unite!

---

*"StrategyOne Labor Day Public Opinion Survey on the American Worker" on the PR newswire on September 3, 2010.

Boring Meetings Suck introduces a radical new approach and premise, and it dares to admit what other books avoid—that every attendee has a right and responsibility to make every meeting productive for all involved. Only when empowered attendees diplomatically speak up and get meetings on track will everyone benefit, instead of suffering in silence as an ineffective facilitator loses control.

What I'm calling for is for you—and everyone you meet with—to become part of the Bore No More! movement, and this book, *Boring Meetings Suck*, is the backbone of that movement.

I'm not encouraging outright mutiny here, and I definitely don't want you to get fired for walking out of all your meetings. I simply want to help make your day more productive. Don't let yet another era pass full of finger-pointing, faultfinding, and miserable meetings. Personally and financially, we simply cannot afford to do so a moment longer.

Fortunately, advanced guidance is here in the Agenda Items on these pages you have in your hands—a book that will revolutionize the new millennium.

Hey, Not *All* Meetings Suck

Please don't get the idea that, in this book, I'm only ranting about poorly run meetings. If I did that, I'd just be another victim blaming everyone and their mother for all the time wasted in meetings.

Let me set something straight right now.

I'm officially and boldly stating this: Meetings can be *awesome*. After all, face-to-face meetings are the lifeblood of

3

thriving organizations. By definition, meetings are the act of people coming together to achieve a common goal through communication and interaction. That "achieving a common goal" is the key to this whole thing. And when meetings are engaging, they accomplish amazing things. They:

- Deliver information that allows team members to excel.

- Foster a spirit of creativity.

- Supply much-needed motivation and incentive.

- Build unity, cohesion, and commitment to a mission.

In contrast, it's those poorly planned, poorly facilitated meetings with poor participation that suck the life out of business, government, and non-profit organizations.

A *great* meeting can provide *great* value, especially when *great* value has been designed into it. Many professional meeting and event planners, executives, cubicle workers, and others have skillful ideas of what to do: They prepare well, engage others, get issues finalized, and end a meeting when it's time for it to end. Their well-run meetings add value to everyone's professional and personal growth as well as to the organization's bottom line.

If you're one of these accomplished meeting planners or facilitators, I commend you and offer you even more amazing advice. I promise you'll find this book *indispensable* in achieving your desired outcomes.

Nothing More Boring Than a Boring Book about Boring Meetings

Yes, this is a book about meetings, but I solemnly promise it's not another boring meeting book. The only thing worse

4

than a boring meeting is a boring book about meetings! Trust me, I know. This is a fun, doable-instead-of-daunting read, so even the busiest of road warriors can dig in and derive value in a few minutes.

In this book, *Boring Meetings Suck*, I want to do more than share my secrets. I want to empower you to take responsibility and make any meeting you attend better, even if it looks hopeless. If it's *truly* hopeless, I'll also let you in on my years of research about how to get out of a meeting without getting fired—an art form in itself.

To speed things along, I've introduced what we at Bore No More! headquarters have christened **Suckification Reduction Devices**—SRDs, for short. They're easy-to-read and even-easier-to-implement ideas that you'll appreciate having when you find yourself stuck in another boring meeting.

You'll see SRDs for facilitators, attendees, presenters and organizers noted at the end of each Agenda Item. They're true gems that can catapult you from a mere participant to a "Get More Out of Meetings, or Get Out of More Meetings" master.

What's in It for You?

I'm on a mission to get everyone on the Bore No More! bandwagon. I want good meetings to be great; I want unnecessary meetings to stop; and when they're not productive, I want to show you how to fix them or get out of them gracefully.

This book is for you if:

- You're a meetings expert looking to improve your already stellar meeting performance and enhance client meetings with new ideas and methods.

5

- Your organization needs an easy reference blueprint for more effective meetings.

- You and your team want to stop wasting time with poorly planned and administered meetings.

- You're willing to step up and take responsibility for every meeting you're in, even if you're not hosting it.

- You're among the millions upon millions who see that boring meetings suck the energy, time, creativity, and even profit out of our organizations—and want to change that.

When you take the Agenda Items to heart, you'll learn:

- How to excuse yourself from a meeting without losing your job.

- Three polite, proactive ways to motivate people to "wrap it up."

- Why you and others should turn your phones *on* in meetings.

- Quips and tips to make your presentation powerful, not pointless.

- Essential elements for planning large meetings or conferences.

- New techniques that will enable you to run "Get In, Get It Done, and Get Out" meetings.

- How to be the hero of your meetings, have people show up on time, participate fully, and applaud your efforts as they return to their desks with extra time in their pockets.

The more people who understand and accept these concepts, the better, so everyone can reap the benefits of using them in meetings.

How Do You Use This Book? Jump in and Read the Agenda Item You Need

Frankly, beyond the first Agenda Item, it doesn't matter where you start reading this book. That's right. Read it completely randomly or out of order if you like. Look at the contents headings. If a particular Agenda Item piques your interest, go for it. Grab what you want when you can use it most.

You'll find *Boring Meetings Suck* to be an essential book that can be referenced at a moment's notice whenever the need strikes. In most cases, the SRDs in each Agenda Item can be used right away, no long deliberation needed. Read an item, pick your favorite SRD, and apply it. Then repeat as needed.

Are You Ready to Make Meetings Rock?

Join other large and small organizations that have made the Bore No More! philosophy their guide. And bring the movement into your office with help from our Bore No More! staff at www.BoreNoMore.com.

As you read *Boring Meetings Suck*, you'll laugh and maybe even cry. My hope is that you'll look at yourself and realize what others have whispered behind closed doors: "this meetings sucks!" And then you'll do something about it.

If you're sick and tired of being sick and tired of boring meetings, heed this advice. Either apply the ideas in this book along with your team and organization and get on with your life, or risk another hundred-plus years of humankind making every kind of technological improvement imaginable yet forgoing one of our greatest strengths—our ability to make meetings *rock* instead of *suck*.

Are you ready?

Agenda Item 2

Better Meetings and Conventions through Technology . . . but *Please* Proceed with Caution

"I would appreciate it, if you would take a moment to please turn off your phones or leave them in the box by the door."

In our technology-laden world, there's basically one response to that request, "Um, you can kiss my . . ."

You want to start your meeting with a twist that will raise some eyebrows? Try this one.

"Hey, everyone, please make sure your phones are out and on."

You don't seriously expect people to go a fraction of a minute without their safety blanket in the form of a phone, do you? Do you really expect them to make continual eye contact with you?

Heck no. Expect them to be interacting in your meeting and to have two digital dialogues going at the same time. So why not concede the point?

In reality, if your meeting is productive and engaging, you won't have random texting that isn't directly related to the function of the meeting. If your meeting is boring, on the other hand, then good luck with that and don't let the door hit you on the way out.

The fascination of instantaneous communication with anyone in the world at any time mixed with the sheer separation anxiety most of us feel when that mobile device is not securely on our hip or in our pocket, is no fault but our own. We've been bred to read e-mail anywhere we are, thanks to our BlackBerrys, and texting is not just a language for teenagers anymore. From the most basic forms of technology in these examples to the most sophisticated and new applications to "enhance our productivity," we are forever either troubled or blessed with technology in our meetings. It all depends on the way you look at it. Just a few years ago I had a different approach. I thought text messaging was a glorified way of passing notes in class like we did in third grade.

Today, texting and other techniques that are readily available in the palms of our hands open the realm of instant information sharing, gathering, and evaluating on a grand scale and with a global reach. This can take idea-generation sessions to new heights, for example. You can poll opinions and solutions, just to mention two of the myriad things current technology can do.

> **Technology is grand stuff. But here's the problem. The meeting organizer or facilitator allows technology to become the meeting instead of enhance it.**

You know the phenomenon well. In our personal lives, we are bombarded with all the new developments and cool things that are supposed to make life better, more productive, and efficient. But too often, all the gadgets and widgets we use force us to cram more and more into an already overcrowded day. We've come to spend more time looking at a digital screen and less time interacting with other humans.

The fact is that it still comes down to us. We make our lives what they are. We make the decisions to use these gadgets to our benefit or simply just to look cool and keep up. Similarly, if we are cramming technology into our general office meetings because it seems like the right thing to do, or if we are trying to replace our ineffectiveness by hiding behind digital distractions, then we need to take a hard look at why we are using them.

If you put together a videoconference with your team in Houston and feel that just because you are "together" as a team you can skip the formalities of a proper agenda and real objectives, then you're sadly mistaken. I see this happen on a regular basis with online and Web-based meetings in which the hosts think the technology of the meeting platform will do the work for them. Result—one sucky meeting! (See Agenda Item 6, "Online or Virtual Meetings Suck.")

Corbin Ball of Corbin Ball Associates, an expert in meeting technologies with more than 20 years of experience, who has been named as one of the "25 Most Influential People in the Meetings Industry" by *MeetingNews Magazine* for four years running, shares with me his position:

> Meeting professionals grapple like everyone else in this ever-changing environment of new advances and uses of technology. It allows us to bring in speakers who may be in other locations and can engage the audience with real-time polling and event feedback. The key is

11

definitely to provide potential to enhance the meeting in a way in which everyone can partake, but not losing sight of the meeting design or outcomes in place of cool technology.

One technology that I, like many others, have made a personal habit of using, in a small way, has been social media. In so many cases, Facebook or Twitter contains fluff: random updates or points that most people couldn't possibly care about. But what if we apply this core technology to a meeting environment? How can we use it to generate new ideas or as a tool to foster creativity? In fact, that's what I did at various times while creating this book. In several chapters, I share actual feedback from various postings on social media sites. I have done it for this chapter, too, by posing this question on Facebook: "What technology in a meeting can you *not* live without?"

I was totally surprised by the answers:

"A ballpoint pen"
"Paper"
"Fresh whiteboard and new markers"
"Digital camera"
"The mute button"
"Giant sticky note pads"
"Good PA system"

I didn't get it at first. Those weren't the answers I was looking for. "No," I Facebooked back, "I said *technology!*"

I wanted another opinion, so I spoke with Wendy Nicodemus, the general manager of Quest Conference and Business Centers, a state-of-the-art meeting and special event facility in Columbus, Ohio. It's an exceptional space with a high-service oriented team, and all the cool technology toys you'd ever want to try.

I asked her "What are people *really* using?"

"Most are still in the PowerPoint and projector mode" Wendy explains. "And we still need to help them understand the importance of a second screen with larger audiences."

I was disappointed. I had hoped to hear that my social respondents and Wendy's clients were using the newest gadgets and high-definition video telepresence units, projectors the size of phones, and Bluetooth pens that digitally transcribe right to your laptop. But they weren't. I realized the honest truth; most people are not using it.

Is this normal? Good? Bad?

If what you are using works and creates effective meetings, then run with it. There may not be a need to implement instruments or devices that may get in the way of real progress. At the same time, there are some core tools and devices that you need to be aware of and prepared for, tools that could seamlessly enhance your ability to Get In and Get It Done. Your ability to integrate technology will all depend on your comfort level with the technology and that of your meeting attendees, as well as on your ability to manage it effectively so it doesn't hinder the progress of your meeting and create the suck factor this book is all about.

Let me share the tip of the iceberg on some core technologies you should be familiar with to plan for and expect in your upcoming meetings. In addition, because I couldn't resist, I'll also give you some ideas you may want to

13

consider for the enhanced and advanced users—and especially the downright daring meeting planners for larger events.

Disclaimer: First, if you're a seasoned technology professional, then this might not entertain you. As mentioned in the introduction, read what you need to and jump to the section that entertains you. Second, let's get real for a moment, shall we? This technology section could be obsolete before *Boring Meetings Suck* even hits the bookshelves. Online platforms and mobile applications proclaiming to make you more effective and productive in your meetings and the planning of such, are being developed and marketed at unbelievable rates in an attempt to capture the almighty dollar.

I like a new web site that is trying to ease the confusion of all the mobile applications available for everyone from your common office meeting organizers to advanced professionals and convention management systems. Check out www.meetingapps.com, the first online portal featuring the most useful mobile applications available to international meeting and event professionals.

Whatever technology you decide to implement, have fun with it and have everyone be a part of it. Experiment. See what works and what doesn't, and keep everything that your meeting attendees respond to well. And always remember, the technology is not in charge, *you* are.

The Very Basics

The following is the easy stuff—what you need to start implementing technology in your meetings. It's basic, so feel free to jump ahead as needed.

Wi-Fi	Broadband access in all meeting spaces should be readily available.
Phones	A better term would be *mobile devices*. They are our personal digital companions more than phones nowadays, and their possible uses in meetings are endless, from custom collaboration applications to note-taking. They are here to stay and to stay on. Live with it and welcome it. With so many ways to use mobile devices, what works best for you?
Texting	You will see references throughout this book to using texting for quick information gathering, meeting updates, and ways to get out of boring meetings. Don't fight it anymore. Use it to your advantage.
Web	Stop printing all the documents for distribution, and instead provide attendees with a Web URL from which they can download and print documents, as they desire. No projector? Place your presentation on the Web and provide attendees with the address. They can follow along on their phones as they wish.
iPad	As the iPhone drove the touch screen phone markets, the iPad is driving the touch screen mobile computing market. Dell is in the game as well with its Streak tablets, and Microsoft has plans of its own. This could very well become the type of mainstream apparatus that changes the face of meetings, just as the PC did in the 1980s.

Enhanced Meeting Technologies
Online Collaboration

I remember my first job in the beginning of the 1990s, in which a shared whiteboard on your network was the cool thing. Multiple users could simultaneously review, edit, or draw on the presentation.

Since then, online collaboration tools have come an incredibly long way in terms of ease of use, functionality, and availability. People can now access Web-based collaboration platforms and meet virtually anywhere they go at any time. Here are a few of my favorites.

Doc sharing: Google Docs and Microsoft Office Live Workspace (among numerous others) allow you to create documents and have many people access and work on them from wherever they are. Your agendas, presentations, spreadsheets, meeting notes, or project updates can be managed simply and for *free*. Try sharing your upcoming agenda for comments, additions, or suggestions about what needs to be accomplished in this meeting.

Basecamp: A leading online project collaboration tool and fantastic system from the company 37Signals. (Also, a cool book from its founders, titled *Rework,* has some great content on "Toxic Meetings.") While not a free system, it's very affordable and packed with features that provide real value for any project team that is meeting virtually or in person on a regular basis.

Web meetings: Wow, too many to mention, but you've likely heard of several of the big players in the market, including WebEx and GoToMeeting. These have become widely used in many situations where planned one-to-many learning meetings, or even ad hoc quick collaboration meetings, are necessary and need screen sharing or collaborative workspace, complete with real-time video capabilities if you so desire. They allow participants to join the meeting and interact from anywhere they can access broadband Internet.

16

Instant Audience Feedback

Not until several years ago were we able to get truly real-time audience feedback without the need for verbal inter-ruptions. "Hey, we can't hear you!" We polled audiences through showing of hands, applause, or surveys and eval-uated their engagement by the snooze factor of the meet-ing (e.g., how many people were snoring). Technology has changed this whether we like or not. And it doesn't just provide instant feedback to the presenter or meeting plan-ner, it broadcasts it to the world.

You've heard of Twitter all right, and people may even be tweeting about your meeting right now. Users have 140 characters in the form of a microblog to share their thoughts, message, or rant. Although I'm on Twitter (@JonPetz), I still find myself struggling to find the time or reason why people would be interested in what I had for lunch. However, in larger meetings and conferences, I find it invaluable for the attendees and the organizing team.

For events, you can follow all the updates if you know the particular event code that uses the # symbol. For exam-ple, "Just finished the keynote at the #EVENT2011 national convention." If you search #EVENT2011 on Twitter, you will see everyone who is tweeting about that event pub-licly. How could this possibly be helpful?

For the organizers, what a great way to communicate to your attendees en masse about changes to programs, bus schedules, or other updates. The downside is that not everyone is listening. You can't rely on this message getting to all attendees.

For vendors at these shows, what a great way to mar-ket. (Overdo it, though, and people will stay clear of you.) Maybe once at a conference, try a tweet using the # tag:

17

"First one to share their top three lessons learned today at the @BoreNoMore booth enters bonus prize drawing (#EVENT2011)."

As an attendee, let me share with you my first eye-opening experience showing the power of Twitter. I was sitting in the audience at the Meeting Professionals International "Meet Different" Conference in Atlanta, Georgia. Hollywood star Ben Stein was on the stage speaking, and his microphone was clipping in and out. I (in an annoyed fashion) tweeted about the challenge of hearing him. Within two minutes there was a tweet from the audio production company (which, of course, has the appropriate # tag for the event in order to track tweets) explaining why this was occurring and what it was doing to fix it. I was amazed. The production company was following the tweets for the event in real time and responded back to me personally—along with everyone else, of course—yet as one person out of thousands in the audience, I felt at peace. I felt I'd been heard and I felt it was being take care of. How about *that* for customer service at a convention!

At the same event, day two, and I'm into only my second day of Twitter. I was previewing the feeds during another keynote. Behind the speaker was this amazing animated graphic of the Earth spinning. A tweet was broadcast: "This spinning globe is making me sick." Remarkably, within 30 seconds it stopped spinning. Without that communication we would probably have heard the typical announcement from the PA system: "Cleanup in aisle 425—we've got a puker."

As a speaker, I expect people to be texting or tweeting to some extent during my presentations, so I share my username (@JonPetz) at the beginning of the presentation, along with the #EVENT tag, if applicable. Although I don't check the search results during the keynote, I know some people who do. If you call out username Doubting Deborah to ask why she thinks your tie conflicts with the colors in your eyes, just imagine her surprise.

Audience Response Technology

While Twitter is communication that isn't planned in many cases, what about opportunities to interact with, engage, and assess the audience on their opinions or status, or to test their understanding of the content you are presenting? That is easily within your reach to implement in small or large meetings, due to the success of the technology and ease of use for participants.

Companies such as Turning Technologies help you create interactive slide presentations that engage audiences and provide them with instantaneous feedback displayed in PowerPoint for all to see. Audience members use a remote-control device supplied by the presenter or simply their Web-enabled phone. If desired, feedback can be anonymous, or it can be set up to track individual user responses while still displaying the answers as a group. Say you want to ask a group of employees what they *really* think about the new employee benefits, avoid the yelling, and have everyone instantly see the response. This can help.

Try text polling. Do you want to poll the audience in real time but don't have the software or hardware to pull it off? Then send people to their phones. (And just think, you used to tell people to turn them off or leave them by the front door. It's okay . . . you didn't know any better.)

Text-style (or SMS) polling is a great way to accomplish this with the help of a provider such as Poll Everywhere or SMSPoll. They create a real-time experience of information exchange at events with attendees' mobile

19

devices and then display audience responses within presentation software or Web applications. Some systems are enabled for response via Twitter or web sites as well. Their functionality is not generally as robust as the features built into the specific handheld polling devices, but you don't need to buy the devices either. And of course, standard messaging rates apply.

Other Enhancing Ideas

Use podcasts. Why not simply have your status meeting as a downloadable audio file that you can dump onto your phone or a memory stick that you can drop into your smart car? Team members can post quick updates on milestones reached or challenges uncovered. Team members set the Real Simple Syndication (RSS) feed to get notified or auto-download anytime a new file is available.

Try YouTube. If people can't attend a meeting and don't have videoconference capability, have them post a video to YouTube. You don't need flashy editing, just keep it simple. Or, as a meeting organizer, create teaser videos for your meetings. Build the anticipation of the energy and excitement of the conference and share it on YouTube.

For the More Adventurous

The following tips are only for those truly comfortable with the advanced technology available. You want to take this stuff step-by-step. If you like the idea of what you read in this section, great, but just know you have to start at whatever point you're most comfortable with and move up from there.

Meeting Mngr Pro: An application now available that I look forward to hearing more about and using personally is Meeting Mngr Pro. Inspired by and designed after the popular Seth Godin (international best-selling author) blog, in which Godin builds his dream effective meeting application, Meeting Mngr Pro is an iPad app to make meetings more interactive by giving people an easy way to participate, create surveys, vote, share documents, and give feedback in real time. The app allows as many iPads as necessary to be connected without the need for an online server or Internet connection for most of the functionalities. While it may drive all of your participants to be looking down instead of up and require everyone to have an iPad, it's destined to be a noteworthy application if it keeps up with the times and feedback suggestions.

Wikis: No doubt you've heard of Wikipedia, the online resource for . . . everything. Why not create your own wiki? It's a collaborative-style web site in which all participants can access data and provide updated information. Your project team can individually post and access all past meeting notes, project updates, or review convention logistics.

Prompster: This is the iPad version of a teleprompter. Give a presentation like the best of them with a working teleprompter in the palm of your hands. A downside is that it's in the palm of your hands and you're not looking at the audience. Check out Agenda Item 5, "Your Presentation Sucks." This may help.

For the Outright Daring

Telepresence, in its simplest form, is the future of what most know as videoconferencing. With full-screen options, true broadcast high-definition quality, and state-of-the-art collaboration software, this technology is amazing to see and use. While advanced room systems can cost hefty amounts, they definitely rank high on the cool factor. How effective they are is based on your skills as a facilitator and user. If you want to "try before you buy," some Starwood and Marriott conference centers are building public suites for rent. Heck, Cisco even has a unit for your home television now.

Geopositioning allows you to log into the conference web site and select particular people you want to meet, companies you want to learn about or network with, and sessions you want to attend. Your name badge does the rest. If you are within a specified distance of your selected person or place, it will notify you. Sherpa Solutions introduced its ActivPassport name badge system, which provides attendees' precise geolocation, to help you find your way on the show floor; you can locate particular booths—and even get user real-time data about other attendees who are currently around them. Yeah . . . really!

Want to see more? The Worldwide Technology Watch (WWTW), an EIBTM initiative started 10 years ago, has become a leading industry program to find the most innovative technology solutions for the meetings and events industry. Check out www.eibtm.com for more information.

Better meetings with better technology. That would definitely be the goal if you're up for the challenge. But also be aware of the suckification that poorly used or abused technology can cause. No matter what newest gadget or software tickles your fancy, it can't be used as an excuse for not getting the job done in terms of meeting the expectations and objectives of your meeting. Ask yourself how technologies can be used to enhance or streamline

22

communication, build engagement, or even increase input in a way that allows the user to maximize efficiency and creative participation. When you have the answer, you find the technology to match.

Always remember, technology isn't the meeting— *you are*!

Agenda Item 3

How to Be a Meeting Superhero . . . in 10 Minutes or Less

I'm not sure if you've been getting the underlying gist of what I've been saying—and if you haven't, then maybe I'm not being direct enough. Yet there's a simple fix to this whole meeting problem: Just don't have them!

That may seem like a dream world, or possibly an un-productive world based on your mind-set. My main point: When in doubt, find, use, and exhaust other possible modes of communication first before requesting the prime-time working hours of the greater population. Remember, poorly run meetings suck because they can suck time, energy, and creativity—and in the end, they can suck the profit out of your organization as well.

If you absolutely, positively, must, must, *must* have a meeting, Agenda Item 3 offers suggestions on how to con-duct meetings that don't suck, that use creativity, that get you in and out of that dang conference room fast, by design.

Part 1, "New Meeting Styles," deals with changing the way you meet. It's about meeting styles designed to put a spark back into your team, to reignite their creativity and participation.

25

Part 2, "Speed Meetings," is my favorite. Hate to spend an hour in a meeting? Then don't. Spend 18 minutes instead and get the same amount done. How cool is that?

So buckle your seat belt and hold onto your shorts, because these ideas just might change your life forever . . . well, at least that part of your day that you so desperately want to change.

Part 1: New Meeting Styles

Everyone loves "new." The newest phones and mobile tablets with solar charging, 3D television, instant coffee being *cool* again, cars that nearly drive themselves, full-wall video-conferencing, and wireless everything.

Why not spruce up your meetings by adding a touch of the *new*—that is, four new meeting styles? Trust me, these ideas will help to combat the boredom!

New Meeting Style 1: "Open House"

Scheduling a meeting time for a group of busy individuals can take more time than actually holding the meeting. Your team has other meetings and events all day; you can't find that 30-minute block of time that synchronizes on everyone's calendar. Ugh!

Regretfully, this will never change in your lifetime. It might be easier if you're looking to schedule a 20-minute "Two 'n Out," (coming up in "Speed Meetings") but when you need an hour or more, good luck.

Ask these clarifying questions: Is this the kind of meeting that needs everyone physically together to share ideas, concepts, or findings? Or is it simply important that you all have that opportunity to comment on, discuss, and share these ideas?

In the good old days when we needed to share ideas and get feedback, we'd send an e-mail and solicit input. That's old-school now. It's also problematic. You'd have to repurpose that information from each e-mail to share with everyone else in an endless loop of comments. Too much time to organize. Bad.

But who says we have to all be stuck together at once? Why not open the meeting space for a specified period and allow participants to share their thoughts *on their own time*? You can set up a space in the conference room that allows people to post information in some way. Good old sticky notes are my favorite, but whiteboards or large writing pads will do. With this setup, people can return later to read what others have posted and then post their own comments, rebuttals, or votes.

The cool part about this? It all happens *on a person's own time*!

If you want to be adventurous, you could set a 15-minute speed meeting of your choice to "Get In and Get Out" with all of your data already in place.

Here's a variation: What about a virtual environment or having team members at various locations? Ever heard of something called *wikis*? (If you're not already using this wonder app, you'll want to after reading the technology discussion in Agenda Item 2.)

If you're not familiar with wikis or don't have the IT resources to set one up, you might try Facebook. Why not set up a fan page? The "wall" and "comment" and "like"

27

features take care of the entire administrative requirements for you. You can post information and comment all day long, *and* you know exactly what came from whom and at what time. Couldn't be much easier or faster to set up.

Ground rules

- Set up a space in your conference room where people can write on whiteboards or post sticky notes. However you decide to post information, make it clear that that's what the space should be used for. Make sure there's an area to post initial data as well as a place to post rebuttals and additional comments.

- Set a time window for the "Idea sharing" or "Comment" phases, when group members are able to input or post their information, rebuttals, or comments. Send your meeting invitation with the times clearly specified and hold firm to them. For example:

  ○ 9 PM–12 PM Place a sticky note with your comments or ideas under the appropriate task challenge.

  ○ 1 PM–4 PM Post your comments on other ideas; each person stick *only* the three gold stars provided on your preferred solutions. No, you can't put *all* your stars on any one solution, and you must use all three stars.

  ○ 4:45 PM–5:00 PM Brief discussion on the most popular solutions. [Variation to the end discussion: Why not take the stairs or do a "Two 'n Out" with the top 10 the next day?]

- State how and where to share information. Send a link to the designated wiki or Facebook page. Or spell out which whiteboard, cubicle, or conference room is being used and how to post information, whether you write in it or simply use sticky notes stuck to the wall under each heading.

- Removing other people's information is not allowed.

- All notes can be anonymous, or each person can use a particular color marker or note. Alternatively, have participants sign their names.

When to use this type of meeting

- Use it when team members are difficult to get together or have offices in remote locations.

- Use it when personal agendas or influence of meeting attendees could get in the way of generating ideas or giving personal opinions.

- Use it when you need to narrow a large number of ideas or gain feedback on existing ideas.

What you need

- Designate specific areas for these tasks.

- Use appropriate materials in each space, as needed.

- Establish a wiki page or set up access to Facebook from your company firewall.

Pros

- People have flexibility in time and schedules.

- Individuals can share ideas in 10 minutes rather than a one-hour meeting that may conflict with another scheduled event.

- You have the ability to start face-to-face meetings or Webinars with all thoughts on the table and visible to everyone. *If you choose this option, you may want to confirm your top three items of discussion ahead of time, based on your group voting technique*. This system can allow anonymity for those who hold back expressing their ideas and opinions in public forums.

Cons

- You may see people all come in at the last minute to write down their ideas, but at least they are doing so on their own time.

- Anonymity suffers if everyone recognizes Jimmy's handwriting.

- Not everyone may choose to participate, so all opinions may not be represented.

New Meeting Style 2: "Pass the Buck"

It's inevitable. You host a meeting and you hear through the grapevine that people don't like it or that they whine about your bad meetings. You also get hit with this in real time if some of your attendees are fans of this book. If they hand you a copy, just know they are only trying to help.

But why should you take all the flack? Bad meetings are everyone's responsibility, so if you manage a team and are getting flack for your meetings, it's time to "Pass the Buck" and let team members take a stab at leading them.

One of my sales managers back in the day, Frank Pacetta (now an executive at Xerox), used to share this with our team: "You can whine, but you darn well better have three suggestions on how you can fix it. Otherwise, stop complaining and bringing everyone else down with you." Go, Frank!

If you're in this position, let the group know what it takes to run the meeting by allowing each member a chance to take charge. Worst case, they will have a far greater appreciation for what it takes to run a meeting. If you're lucky, they'll learn how tough it can be when no one participates; they'll know how it feels when no one comes prepared.

Ground rules

- Lead the first meeting yourself. This sets the structure for your objectives and allows you to set the tone for the project team. Then "Pass the Buck" after that.

- In the first meeting, distribute the calendar of upcoming meeting organizers and facilitators. Decide who will lead each meeting so they can each pick their dates. Unilaterally informing people they will "lead tomorrow's meeting" is simply not cool and leads to angry people staying late to get ready. Bad.

- Provide the scheduled leader with your format and suggestions if asked, but put the majority of the organization and responsibility on that person. Remember, you aim to mix up the leadership styles and format as well as getting others to own the responsibility for the meeting itself.

- Don't force leaders into processes or procedures. Allow other methods, styles, and processes to bubble to the top. Give them guidance and support, as needed, before the meeting.

- You've given others the task to lead, so when it's meeting time, allow them to do it.

When to use this type of meeting

- Obviously, this works best with a group that meets regularly.

- If you are in an equal peer-to-peer working relationship and you demand that each person lead a meeting, it could be met with a defensive "you're-not-my-boss" attitude. This meeting type tends to work best when the senior person explains that by each member hosting a meeting and by everyone working together, the team will meet with success.

- If you're part of a volunteer organization or association, you can't force people into leading. Offer it up, but don't require it.

What you need

- Choose a method to schedule and distribute the meeting planner or facilitator information.

- You can start with a template or leave that up to the creativity of each individual.

Pros

- You may learn something! What a concept. Watch how other team members react to what meeting leaders do successfully and unsuccessfully. Take notes and adopt the ideas you like.

- Attendees will realize leading a meeting isn't as easy as they thought. Maybe they'll start cutting you slack for your own lack of effectiveness.

- Different leaders gather different participation from attendees. If a drama club member leads one meeting and a volleyball player leads another, they'll bring different ideas and skill sets to the table, which will open the meeting to different kinds of discussion. Oh, and be prepared—you may finally get some feedback from Silent Susan.

- Be ready for better teamwork and understanding of others' personalities and workflow styles. If you see Visual Violet using all visual elements in place of text, it shows how she likes to communicate. On her next employee evaluation, you have an idea of how you can communicate more effectively with her. The better we understand how to communicate effectively with someone, the better we can tackle our objectives in a stable and organized way.

- You may witness firsthand what *doesn't* work.

Cons

- Unorganized Ursula may really have poor skills in leading a meeting or may never have done it before. If you still have overall responsibility for the effectiveness of the team and meeting, be prepared to step in and help . . . and I mean it. Prepare before the meeting. You know your team, and therefore you know who might need extra help.

- If you do step in, your team members may feel underappreciated or that they are not meeting your expectations. Be careful to give guidance and answer questions, but do not tell them what to do.

- If you do try to take over during the meeting time, be prepared for a negative effect—and not only in the current meeting. All upcoming meeting leaders will assume you'll do the same thing to them. They'll anticipate you'll come in with plans to take over their meeting, and so they'll prepare less.

New Meeting Style 3: "Stand It Up"
It's unanimous. We come into the meeting room, sit in the chairs, lean back, and go into *meeting mode*. You know what I'm talkin' about?

33

It's that "I'm-going-to-be-here-for-at-least-an-hour-so-I-might-as-well-get-comfortable" feeling—the same one that can change your brain from a productive, task-oriented mode to one of being a barely breathing body taking up space.

There's an easy fix. Change it up! Take away common elements that are in the standard meeting environment. Don't allow any slouch-back-and-relax mode to take over. Instead, keep all things up and active. Simply put, keep 'em standing.

Here's how: Have a designated meeting space or conference room that has no table or chairs. You literally meet standing up. No need to bring your laptop, because there's no setup for any presentation or slides. You use what's in the room for quick collaboration or idea generation.

With this style, your meeting length will be finely tuned—about the amount of time people are willing to stand and bear it. Otherwise, they vote with their feet . . . and just walk out.

Perhaps you're part of an e-mail dialogue with several people discussing how to implement a new piece of software code, but you differ on how to best proceed. It's time to come out of your Bat Cave, meet in person, "Stand It Up," and talk until everyone agrees on the best method.

Then it's back to the Bat Cave, Batman!

Ground rules

- Lose the conference room table.

- Lose the chairs.

- Have a large whiteboard, chart, or full-wall chalkboard for notes.

- No laptops allowed, as you have no place to put them. However, communication on phones and handheld digital devices is allowed and absolutely encouraged. (Yes, you can text standing up.) Quickly source comments and feedback in this manner. (Oh, and no need to invite those who are needed for only one quick piece, as discussed under Agenda Item 4, "The Overinvitation Sucks.")

When to use this type of meeting

- Ad hoc stand-up meetings work perfectly to flush out quick ideas and move forward. No need to sit for 30 minutes and enter boring meeting mode when you can each sketch or detail your idea on the wall.

- When you think a meeting might take an hour, yet it really only requires 15 minutes, move it to the stand-up collaboration area.

What you need

- Find a conference room or other common space dedicated to this purpose.

- Have collaboration equipment or technology ready and usable at a moment's notice. Try the full-wall whiteboards or digital collaboration (smart) boards that record all your doodling, notes, and details, and then save them to a file or print them remotely. Or just keep it simple with paper and pens that won't be hijacked from that area.

Pros

- People who are standing get moving quickly with their thoughts, especially when sitting back and relaxing is not an option.

- It's effective for a 5-minute quick talk as well as a 45-minute get-together. People sit way too much during their workday, anyway.

- It's easy for others to quickly pop in or out of this kind of meeting to deliver a thought, a comment, or a piece of data.

Cons

- If your stand-up meeting addresses a complicated matter, it may take a long time to work through—longer than people want to stand.

- Some people simply feel lost without their computers and spreadsheets.

- Many people will want to use the same space at the same time. Stand-up collaboration areas could take over traditional conference rooms for quick meetings. So plan for multiple rooms or spaces once you begin using this in your company. You could find the trend catching on quickly and teams adoring it.

New Meeting Style 4: "Triple T Your Way to New Ideas"

"Good evening everyone. If you would, kindly take a minute to turn your phones *on*!"

Remember when brainstorming sessions included only six people in the room, who most often stared at each other after a few items were mentioned? What if we could open this discussion to hundreds, if not thousands, of people?

Just a few years ago, texting was thought to be similar to the old-school technique of passing notes in class—notes scribbled about the boring teacher or the cute sixth grader across the room. You could plan a whole scenario

36

for interaction with those notes. Texting, when it first came out, made it easy to vent frustrations about meetings. If you got caught, well, you risked the same punishment you did from your teachers of old.

Today, this is no longer a question. Whether you're an exceptional meeting host and presenter or a terrible one, your meeting attendees *will be engaged* in digital technology and interactions. How can you play this to your favor?

You really can hold a meeting entirely on electronic devices. Basically, it's the "if-you-can't-beat-'em-join-'em" mentality. If people want to be on their devices, then hold the meeting there! Learn to "Triple T" a meeting with texting, Twittering, and other technologies!

When to use this type of meeting

- Use it when you are looking for idea generation or feedback on a publicly known or accepted topic.

- Try it when you have the ability to seek guidance or feedback on noncomplicated items. People won't read long e-mails, posts, or tweets. You want people to be able to read quickly and give you instant feedback. So text your team members a question, poll, or survey item and let them forward the text and start posting, blogging, and tweeting about it. Then sit back and let the answers, comments, opinions roll in.

What you need

- A team of people with basic texting skills and social media accounts. (You hope they have some friends as well.)

- Some Gen Y and Millenial team members who are helpful and will bring a whole new spirit to the meeting. This is how they learned to communicate, so tap into that resource!

- Choose a method to share the responses, feedback, or information with your internal team. Possibly establish a product or fan page where all links point to respond. Or send them to a link on SurveyMonkey for all answers, or to a #tag for Twitter, or to a discussion topic on LinkedIn to post queries. Worst case, the sender reposts on the group page.

Ground rules

- The meeting takes place at a specified time of day or throughout an entire day, but attendees stay in their offices or cubicles.

- If you want more of a competitive feel, then meet in a specified location and make it a game to see who can get the most feedback the fastest or who can get to a predetermined goal first. Then have a way to reward the winner. Request that everyone bring their devices of choice and be ready to roll. You may want to have other things planned while the "wait" portion (the time after you post and wait for responses) of this meeting takes place.

- Be prepared to tap into your personal and professional network in a fast "dialing-for-dollars" manner.

- Have an incentive for the person who gets the most texts, retweets, posts, or other kinds of feedback from the exercise. Set the rules on the quality of the feedback or ideas.

- Suggest a time frame for these responses. Build urgency into the feedback.

Pros

- What would have been a light drizzle of activity with five people has now become a true brainstorming session with people from many walks of life. You lose the groupthink that often plagues teams.

- Offer all of those who respond a chance to win a small prize. Best new idea wins!

- As the facilitator, try offering a prize for attendees who share the most feedback, "likes," or other ideas generated from outside sources. Allow them to also share this with their network. Friends *want* to see you win and share in that restaurant gift card (or whatever the prize).

- It's one more way of reaching out to clients or prospects and allowing them to feel a part of the process and direction of the services you offer. You're listening to them.

- Even though the time frame may have ended, you'll still receive late entries that could deliver great ideas.

- Undoubtedly, you'll get great ideas from friends who are trapped in their sucky meetings and looking for something to do.

Cons

- The information or ideas *must* be openly public. You don't want negative information or content that puts your organization in a bad light.

- Figure that 90 percent may not respond. Nonetheless, when polling thousands of people on Facebook, LinkedIn, or Twitter, 50 new free ideas with 10 good ones is a big win!

- Take the time to check with your IT department to make sure you are able to access these social media or personal sites. The results from these sources can be astounding.

- And of course . . . standard messaging rates apply.

None of these meeting suggestions is for the faint-hearted. It takes courage to step out of old patterns and change. It also takes a willingness to fall flat on your face once in a while. I'm mostly being figurative here, but you will run into the occasional tumble on the stairs because you're trying something new.

However, if you do make an effort to change meeting styles, your team might be more forgiving when you call a regular old (boring) meeting. Or you may find these ideas make your meetings so productive that you'll wonder why you didn't do something like this years ago. (Be warned, you may cringe when you have to attend meetings run the old-fashioned way.)

Part 2: Speed Meetings

The backbone of the Bore No More! movement is all about "get it done" so you can get on with the real work of the day. What does everyone crave? *More time.* Here are three surefire, speedy ways to gain time.

Speed Meeting Type 1: "Two 'n Out"

Are you a fan of the popular ESPN-TV show *Pardon the Interruption*? If you've never seen this program, let me briefly explain its format. Two hosts debate over a hot list of newsworthy sports items of the day. They're allowed two minutes per topic—that's it. It's fast-paced, full of quick wit, and highly entertaining.

Apply that same concept to your meetings and those days of someone dragging on are gone. You'll be surprised at how much can get done in only two minutes! Limiting the time meeting attendees can speak forces them to get straight to what matters most. Try it and you'll see what kinds of fireworks get sparked. Be sure to set ground rules to which all participants agree before you even start this meeting. Suggested meeting time: no more than a 20-minute meeting with a 5-minute wrap (if needed). Put the "less-is-better" rule into effect.

Ground rules

- Allow two minutes for each participant who needs to share information, provide updates about sales, projects, or status, or otherwise contribute—absolutely no more time and no interruptions within those two minutes. If people interrupt, cut them off. If the speaker finishes under the time limit, give your applause.

- Follow these two-minute segments back-to-back, or interject a one-minute question-and-answer (Q&A) session. No more! Keep it short and focused.

- Assign a note taker to detail all milestones, action items, and follow-up necessary.

- Distribute these ground rules well in advance so attendees can plan accordingly.

When to use this type of meeting

- Use it anytime you can't afford to get off topic and need to complete your meeting in a short time frame. This keeps attendees focused on the essential items that are important to them and need to be known by the others. Skip all the fluff that "takes the

41

dog off the leash" or complicates the stated objectives of the meeting.

- Works fabulously well for status and update meetings held regularly and when attendees need a quick glimpse at the overall project status.

What you need

- Appoint a timer, a facilitator, and a note taker with strong related skills.

- Ideally, have a countdown timepiece so speakers can see the amount of time they have remaining.

Pros

- This style is highly effective for project and status meetings, sales meetings, or pitch, analysis, or feedback meetings. If attendees can't get the meat of your message within two minutes, they'll quickly learn to do so, especially as the speakers' abilities to deliver succinct messages improve.

- It's fun and creates excitement. Once it's established as a recurring meeting type, people love it and look forward to it!

Cons

- Sorrowful Sally or Downer David may have hurt feelings if they're not being heard or believe they aren't important enough to have more than two minutes.

- The first time you try this, there may be a bit of a learning curve. Ease into it if starting a new series of project meetings. Team members will understand it quickly and come prepared if you facilitate the meeting effectively. That is a guarantee!

Speed Meeting Type 2: "Step It Up"

Who wrote the rule on meetings taking place in a conference room?

Do you want people to stop rambling?

Do you want people to get to the point?

Then take their breath away—literally. It's time to take to the stairs!

If we could combat three of the biggest issues that plague our society today—energy consumption, health and obesity challenges, and *boring meetings*—this one would do it all!

In "Step It Up" meetings, you burn calories, save electricity, and create more engaging and focused meetings. A perfect meeting trifecta!

Ground rules

- Each meeting participant has exactly one flight of stairs to make their pitch or status update (or two flights, or as many flights as predetermined by your group).

- Time begins when the first speaker hits the first step and ends when the last person reaches the landing of the agreed-upon level.

- Similar to the "Two 'n Out" style, you can elect to have a Q&A session on the landing.

When to use this type of meeting

- It's most effective with small groups when sharing of information or a quick discussion can appropriately replace long-winded answers and discussions.

- Ad hoc meetings work great here as well. In place of Michael from NBC-TV's *The Office* yelling, "Conference room—five minutes!" tell your team, "Ground floor—five minutes!"

- How about using it when you're brainstorming how to respond to a component in a Request for Proposal (RFP)? Or coming up with topic ideas for your next conference? Or deciding what types of awards to give presenters at your next conference?

- You name it! No really, you name it. Are you naming the new widget, device process, software, team? This is the perfect meeting setting to discuss this kind of stuff at a fast pace.

What you need

- You'll need a building with stairs—the more floors and stairs, the better.

- You'll want a voice recorder or voice memo app on your phone to record the ideas.

- Find a good facilitator to police attendees who may be stepping over the line. I mean that in terms of controlling people from talking beyond their given set of stairs.

- You also need attendees who are in relatively good physical condition to begin with!

Pros

- Scientifically speaking, this method will physically put new life into your meetings. When your heart beats fast, it pumps additional blood to the brain and your energy levels go up. People tend to think more clearly and speak more directly because the blood flow stimulates brain neurons that simply weren't active in PowerPoint prison. Gee, wonder why?

- When you've finished stair climbing, you'll have endorphins pumping through your body—complete with that "natural high"—for some time after your exertion. As a bonus, it's productive time to get your action items done in a creative manner.

- No PowerPoint!

- It's fun to cheer on Stallin' Stan to reach the next landing so the group can stop listening to Ramblin' Randy's babble.

- No PowerPoint! (Wait, did I already say that?)

Cons

- High heels.

- You can't force this on people; if you do, you risk violating the "creating a hostile work environment" clause of every human resources handbook and state legislature.

- Team members might already know what Jawbone Jimmy will say, so you have your team *run* up the stairs and leave him with a mere 10 seconds to speak. (Maybe this is a pro.)

- Just like the roller coasters—If you are experiencing back, heart, or neck problems, or are pregnant, we don't recommend you ride.

- Skyscrapers!

Let's hear from you and see who wins the award for the longest "Step It Up" meeting. Just by trying, I guarantee you'll have some energy-filled team members.

Option: You like the idea but it's not right for your team? Bail out and take the elevator, but shift the ground rules. Yes, you'll lose some *big* health benefits, but this still gives you an option.

Don The Idea Guy Snyder, a creative consultant who rescues those in need of innovative ideas, offers a great variation for those working on different floors. Everyone takes the elevator to the top floor and rides the elevator down, disembarking at their respective floors. You get to talk only as long as the elevator is moving between floors.

Speed Meeting Type 3: "I Gotta Use It"

As a sales manager, this one has long been my favorite among favorites. However, use it with discretion.

I base this name on my wife Stacey's and my longtime friend David's "I Gotta Use It" playful banter when one of them needs to use the restroom. Get the point?

The rule for this speed meeting type is straightforward: When the first person leaves the room for a bathroom break, the meeting is over. If you want your group to make a decision *before everyone leaves the room,* then maybe this is your trick of the trade.

46

You may combine this with the ground rules for "Two 'n Out," or apply "I Gotta Use It" in conjunction with any meeting style. Are you still game?

Ground rules

- Provide a glass of water for each person, to be consumed at the beginning of the meeting.

- The meeting is over when the first person leaves to go to the restroom.

- Alternatively, you can set the length of the meeting by the amount of water each person is provided and expected to consume. One glass of water could equate to a one-hour meeting, but a jug of water will have your attendees hopping in 20 to 30 minutes.

When to use this type of meeting

- Use it anytime you want.

What you need

- Provide water and a glass for each person.

- Maybe have a bucket on hand—just in case.

Pros

- Your meeting will end!

- This can be applied to nearly any meeting type.

- You can control the time limit by how much water is consumed.

Cons

- You can't really *make* people drink water.

- It's definitely not for all company cultures or teams.

47

- Consult your legal department and human resources prior to use. Author is not responsible for improper use or accidental substitution of adult beverages.

- It's quite easy to do the chicken dance and fake your way to the restroom, hence ending the meeting.

Agenda Item 4

Why Everyday Office Meetings Suck . . . Skip This and You're Screwed

So many people constantly complain about lost productivity and how it affects the bottom line. But what's *really* to blame?

The biggest culprit of the billions lost to businesses comes from everyday general office meetings—the impromptu team, sales, update, and project meetings. They're the meetings we dread, complain about, and endure while wishing we could be elsewhere (like doing our *real* jobs). In fact, these impromptu (and annoying) meetings, which I've attended a thousand times over, drove me to create the *Boring Meetings Suck* concept and the first version of this book. Many years later, where are we? In those intervening years, *nothing has changed*. In fact, the boring meeting syndrome has gotten worse.

Why? Because our bosses and companies expect more from us than ever before. We feel stressed because we've learned to force more work into already packed schedules. Now insert these inexcusable wastes of time you call "your meeting" and the negative vibe gets bigger than ever.

So what do we do? We stay late, get up early, drink fancy, high-priced coffee and energy drinks, and complain. Just so we can keep up, we use mobile devices to carry our work everywhere—and I mean everywhere! (While on vacation, have you secretly checked your e-mails in the bathroom so your family members won't see you doing it? Yup, me too!)

Yet after all this stress, are we addressing the root cause of lost production? No. The fact is that most workers (yes, that could be read as *you* or your boss) have never been taught the basics of facilitating a meeting that won't suck the life out of everyone within earshot.

Therefore, if you decide a standard meeting type is right for you, then implement the following core small-meeting elements to improve your time management skills. More than that, doing so will improve the culture in your organization, your relationships with coworkers and bosses, and even the bottom line. (If you're putting together a large meeting for a team gathering or company outing, you'll find even more help in Agenda Item 7, "Big Meetings Suck Even Bigger"—and ain't *that* the truth?!)

Your Preparation Sucks

No doubt you've stepped into a meeting and quickly learned (as if you couldn't tell by the communication you received) that it has no structure or stated goal to accomplish. It's one of those "I-just-thought-we-could-all-talk-about-it" proceedings, or it's a meeting that leads to scheduling another meeting. On top of it all, you stew while the meeting host fumbles to gather everyone's attention, then loses control to Comic Carl and Sidewinder Sam, who bring up crazy ideas and delay the inevitable break from this monolithic meeting style.

50

It's the type of meeting you don't have to prepare for and can show up for anytime you want. For those people who don't care about their time or productivity, it actually provides welcome intrusions to their busy week. What a great way to burn away productive hours! Of course, if enabling team members to engage socially is the intended result, well then carry on.

So much of the value of *any* meeting, though, can be achieved before the meeting event starts. It's up to the facilitators to plan and prepare a meeting or to pay the price of what can happen when they don't. Chances are, you can relate to occurrences like these:

- Attendees become disgruntled because of lack of focus and process.

- Attendees resolve they won't come back to this facilitator's meetings.

- Attendees bring nothing to the table in terms of ideas, content, or questions . . . and don't participate in any way.

- Attendees vote with their feet. (Yup, they just walk out.)

- The facilitator is forced to schedule future meetings because this one has accomplished nothing.

- Everyone's time is completely wasted (and time costs money).

- Meetings run away in multiple directions, but no resolutions are reached.

How can you avoid all this suckiness? By planning. *Anything* worth attending is worth taking time to prepare for. If you're the meeting organizer, know that even taking one minute to review key things before the start of an impromptu or ad hoc meeting can prove invaluable in your overall feeling of accomplishment.

What's the most important prep activity? Clearly stating the goal for the meeting, writing it down, and sharing it with others. Don't forget the other parts—like arriving early to check the meeting location and confirm you have everything you need (and that what you have is in working condition). This can prevent embarrassing, time-wasting recovery actions like looking for markers that mark or replacing a broken speakerphone at the last minute.

If you think preparation relates only to the meeting organizer, think again. All attendees must prepare, too. If you complain about a poorly run meeting and do nothing to change it, then shame on you. Be sure to add your talent and intelligence to the discussion at hand. Get beyond your own purpose for being there and contribute to the group discussion so you help everyone to be more productive with his or her time. Show up prepared and you can finish faster than planned. And who knows? Maybe the goals attained at this meeting will surpass everyone's expectations.

Sound simple? It is. The suggested Suckification Reduction Devices (SRDs) that follow shouldn't come as a surprise to you.

Still, why do so many people avoid the basic concept of planning when its absence contributes greatly to frustration and lost productivity? Maybe it's human nature to be lazy about it. Maybe it's simply not knowing what they don't know. If laziness describes you, stop messing with everyone else's time and do some prep work! If you simply don't know how, then beef up on what to do; most preparation isn't difficult and can be done quickly.

The following core activities can save you the embarrassment of an ill-prepared meeting and its lack of productivity. More important, they'll prepare you to conduct a focused, goal-oriented, and productive meeting.

Facilitator SRDs

- Know your purpose. Simply put, if you can't clearly identify in verbal and written communication *why* you're calling this meeting, then don't call the meeting!

- In advance of the meeting, clearly state and communicate the desired outcomes to all invited parties so they'll have a focused goal in mind when they walk in.

- As soon as the meeting starts, clearly articulate your purpose again. Identify your desired outcomes *and* your dream outcomes ahead of time. If you don't know them, then you have nothing to shoot for. Worse, you don't even know when you're finished with the meeting! Here's an example:

  - *Meeting purpose:* Discuss the options for presenting an updated proposal for client XYZ to meet its cost constraints.

  - *Desired outcome:* Three solutions. Present one primary solution and, as a backup, prepare two alternative solutions that feature more cost-cutting measures.

- *Dream outcome:* Unanimous acceptance of a primary solution, which is then presented to the client and accepted. This calls for a bonus!

- Communicate to all attendees exactly what you expect from them. Provide any data, reading, or necessary information they'll need ahead of time; don't distribute it when they arrive. Everyone being prepared is the goal!

- Arrive early and ready the meeting space or conference room. No one wants to see you plug in your laptop and test the audio *after* the meeting should have started.

- Plan what you'll need to have in the conference room or meeting space. Does the chart have enough paper? Do you have the proper markers, and do they work well? Is the room temperature set for 2 people or 20? Are there enough chairs? Too many? Too few?

- If you meet your planned *desired outcome* sooner than you thought, either go for your *dream outcome* or end the meeting early. No need to keep it going.

Attendee SRDs

- Reread the details of the meeting invitation when you get it, or at least 24 hours in advance. If you read it just before you walk in, it diminishes your opportunity to put in any quality thinking time.

- If your name is on the agenda, be prepared to speak. Don't fall into the trap of showing up and then realizing you needed to graph your milestones or share data you left at your desk.

Get Out!

Realistically, if the facilitator is unprepared, he or she won't even know whether you show up—and might even second-guess having invited you! What should you do? Go back to your office to retrieve items that should have been requested in the first place. While you're in your office, text the facilitator that you've been delayed by another call. Be sure to give your permission for the meeting to move on without you, or else your peers (who are helplessly trapped and mad about further delays) will deliver paybacks!

Having No Agenda Sucks

Meetings with no agendas are like road trips with no maps. They can be fun and spontaneous, and you never know where you might end up. This no-structure approach felt great when my brother Tim and I headed down to Panama City for spring break in college, but it flat-out sucks when talking about a productive meeting.

If you have a stated purpose for your meeting, the agenda will naturally follow as part of your preparation. If you plan to conduct a meeting that encompasses other people's time, then it deserves to have serious thought put into it. An agenda doesn't have to be complex. Rather, it has to guarantee your understanding that you need to create one!

I confess, I find it a tad alarming I have to address such an essential meeting concept here. But the fact is that *most people still don't understand the basics of an agenda*. They either don't take the time to create one or don't know how.

I've often been asked, "Why is an agenda essential when, for example, it's the same four people working through the changes in a proposal? In such a case, is an agenda really necessary?" You bet it is! Otherwise, your group meeting has no form, no structure, and no idea of what should take place. This in turn leads you down the path of multiple sucky meeting types as discussed in Agenda Item 6. And no one likes sucky meetings. *No one.*

On the flip side, you might have created an ineffective agenda and sent it to attendees. When that happens, people simply won't come prepared because they don't know *what* the desired outcomes of the meeting should be. Well, at least you deserve an "atta girl" or "atta boy" for *setting* an agenda.

Preparing even the most basic agenda will save time, frustration, and conflict while increasing engagement and participation. Remember, agendas are not the meeting notes; they are a map of the process to reach your goal.

If you're new to agenda making—and even if you aren't—consider these basics when you create an agenda for your next meeting.

Facilitator SRDs

- Clearly identify desired outcomes and common objectives.

- State the precise date, time, and location; set start and end times.

- Assign a specific amount of time for each agenda item, building in breaks if needed.

- Include time to review action items in a recap session at the end. If you don't, follow-up items may not get documented and acted on.

- Because you want people to participate, schedule them into the agenda. Nothing says "you'd better be prepared" like having the person's name listed to give a plan update or minipresentation, even if it's only one or two minutes long.

- Include supporting or required reading in your agenda. State whether it should be read or reviewed before the meeting or simply brought along.

- Place your most important items first. If you don't get to the other topics, this still leaves you accomplishing the most important issues in the meeting.

- Make sure invited attendees have a final agenda in hand *within 24 hours* of the meeting. Allow more time when a more formal or detailed agenda is required.

- Ask that comments, additions, or suggested changes to the agenda be made by a specified time. *Make this clear in all your premeeting communications.* Why? This gives you greater ability to control tangents and identify challenges ahead of time. It also opens the door for attendees to get or give any additional value they deem necessary.

- Make sure to include rebuttal time for agenda items that could require debating.

- Communicate any agenda changes in advance to all attendees, with any necessary invitation, preparation, or planning points adjusted.

- Include your contact information for comments or questions.

57

- If the meeting is called for within 24 hours and you have no idea what's it's about, then ask. Send a simple e-mail with a subject line similar to this: "Requesting meeting agenda and objectives for tomorrow at 2:01."

- If it's a surprise to see your name in the agenda, make sure you are clear about what's expected of you. If you're not, contact the organizer. Walk in with a clear idea of your role in the meeting.

- If a start time is posted but not an end time, request one. (This happens because of lack of experience or forgetfulness on the meeting planner's part.) Kindly remind the facilitator that you have other issues to deal with that day and want to plan accordingly.

Get Out!

When I was a sales VP in Columbus, Ohio, Jim, our president, started a saying he called the "Jon Petz Rule," meaning, "If you want Jon to show up to your meeting, you'd better send him an agenda."

Similarly, I give you permission to name a rule like this after yourself. It's one way to prevent people from wasting your time by inviting you to so-called meetings that have no stated purpose.

Once you're in the meeting and see that its objectives have been met, don't let it take on a new life with fresh topics. To wrap it up, state your personal follow-up items, thank the facilitator, and get out.

Undoubtedly, an agenda can and will change. It's an important living document that controls the flow of communication, the timing of presentations, and the overall structure. Nike trademarked the concept well: "Just do it."

Your Follow-Up Sucks

My message here can be stated quickly: Be accountable for your stated actions and do what you say you are going to do.

Wouldn't it be a perfect world if this happened every time? Hold on . . . let me just sit in peace and dream about that for a moment. Aah . . . can you feel the excuses, lack of organization, missed priorities, deadlines, and responsibilities gently floating away?

No? Me neither!

Perhaps it's written somewhere that it's against the rules to live in a utopian world of people doing what they promise every time, on time.

Considering that basic meeting preparation is frequently an afterthought, what are the chances of departing attendees actually taking action on all the items discussed? It can happen, don't get me wrong. But it sure can be difficult if you don't build an environment that's conducive to holding people accountable.

The solution? Implement a simple process that enables you to:

- Document the meeting decisions, action items, or responsibilities.

59

- Assign people, teams, or resources to those items.

- Set deadlines or milestones for their completion.

- Have all this information readily available to those who need it.

- Identify a method to confirm items that have been completed.

That's it. A few simple steps to help people stop "talking the talk" and start "walking the walk" instead of leaving empty promises on the conference room table.

While you can't babysit people to get things done, the following SRDs may help facilitate the process.

Facilitator SRDs

- Identify who will document the meeting or keep minutes at the start of the meeting or before. Keep in mind that recording minutes is a skill itself; if you assign someone who has poor note-taking skills, you'll have notes that suck. (Hmmm. "Meeting Minutes Suck." That's for the next edition of *Boring Meetings Suck.*) Having more than one note taker is great; sometimes all attendees will take their own notes. Fabulous!

- Create a Meeting Minutes Map for your team by establishing a consistent method of taking notes no matter who the scribe is. Create a basic template and distribute it so everyone has it and understands it.

- Color-code the notes. Develop a map legend on a shared server, or use whatever template is available.

The map legend identifies common symbols, formatting, colors, or highlighting for specific functions. They should be used by all note takers. Color coding can save a tremendous amount of time when skimming the notes later. It keeps a consistent feel to your minutes and alleviates hardships over discerning what was typed or what meaning was intended.

- Keep the legend simple so it's easy to use. Try this:

  ○ Put action items in bold or red text.

  ○ Name those responsible after the action items (in parentheses).

  ○ Underline decisions that are made.

  ○ Put items discarded for another time in blue.

  ○ Identify other common themes or elements in your meeting.

- During the wrap-up, confirm that everyone heard and agreed to the same thing.

- Plan time in the agenda for the wrap-up—a key component. Review all action items, due dates, and assignments, along with any planned next steps or milestones for the group. Don't send people away feeling confused about their responsibilities or about when to report their findings. Not all attendees hear a discussion in the same way, and it can lead to everyone feeling frustrated. That's why doing a recap is critical.

- Distribute or post minutes as quickly as possible following the meeting. Out of sight means out of mind.

- Make minutes from past meetings readily available. They'll be easy to understand because you used

61

your Meeting Minutes Map and corresponding map legend.

Attendee SRDs

- As part of the Bore No More! movement, don't allow any meeting to wrap up without a firm understanding of what was accomplished—even if the answer is *nothing*, and no follow-up tasks were determined. If the facilitator at any meeting you attend doesn't confirm the progress toward the meeting's goal, then it's your job to speak up and take charge. Who would go against you when you say something like this: "Before we bail, based on my notes, I'm confirming that David is responsible for meeting with Facilities to allow access to the building at that time. Sue has the caterer and menu, and I'm in charge of contacting our meeting planner about the decor and entertainment. We'll confirm all logistics next week, same time, for a final confirmation. Anything I missed?"

- Always document your own action items so you can confirm what is presented at the wrap-up. Otherwise, you may be on the hook for more than you thought!

- Afraid someone isn't taking notes? Ask the facilitator *at the beginning* where the notes will be posted following the meeting. By doing so, you may also be volunteering for the job, but then at least you know it will get done.

- If you come away with action items from the meeting, do them! ("Just do it.") If you won't have them finished in time or to the extent you'd initially planned, communicate that to the stakeholders in a timely way—not at the last minute.

Get Out!

If you're in a group that continues to have meetings with no follow-up, rest assured. Eventually, they will stop with the "no follow-up" behavior because their jobs will be gone. If your meetings are led this way, then it's time to find new team members who will protect your assets.

If you're invited to a meeting that rehashes the same old things (see "Déjà Meetings Suck" under Agenda Item 6) because the facilitator and/or others didn't have time to complete the follow-up, I suggest sending an update via e-mail or other public means. Don't let the organizer call a meeting just to have a meeting where everyone responds with an in-process report.

No doubt you're faced with an ever-increasing medley of items on your to-do list in both your professional and personal lives. Prioritizing schedules to accomplish what's in your own hierarchy of needs is up to you. However, if you're running or attending a meeting, at least be willing to establish a process for identifying items that require follow-up, and state who is accountable for them. And as far as getting it all done—good luck with that! I just hope you don't have too many other meetings in line for the day.

Scheduling a Meeting Sucks

Boring Meetings Suck law: The more people needed to attend a meeting, the more conflicting appointments they have on their calendars. It's like the math problem from hell: If Janet is busy from 8 to 10 on Monday, Tuesday, and Friday, and Bill is available from 9 till noon on those days, but Mark and Judy are both at a trade show in Dallas on Tuesday, Wednesday, and Thursday, and Louise is in training all week . . . how long will it take them to schedule a 30-minute block of time to meet in person?

It's a trick question, of course. The meeting will never happen. The project about which they were to meet will stutter, stall, and completely stop. Each group member will point the finger at another when telling his or her boss why the project goal wasn't met. And they'll all be exactly right and exactly wrong at the same time.

Ever try to organize a night out with your friends? Our family plans a monthly game night with a few other couples. Among three couples and eight kids, everyone juggles a schedule of commitments: project deadlines, performance gigs, keynotes in various cities, family business, soccer games, favorite TV shows, business trips, clubs, and committees—the list is long. The wives are Facebooking back and forth for a week to find a date that just might work. Even then, something often pops up at the last minute to prevent someone from attending. And we're getting together just for *fun*!

Now think about organizing a group event that *no one* wants to attend—*your meeting*. Participants desperately search for ways to avoid sitting in that "bored" room. I know people who have called on sickly relatives to see how poorly they felt, "just in case" there might be a funeral they'd have to attend . . . instead of attending *your meeting*.

Here are ideas about what you can do.

Facilitator SRDs

- Turn to meeting-scheduling tools that might be available in your internal organizational system or even in Outlook or Lotus Notes. Do some homework before reaching out to have people tell you what you could have discovered for yourself.

- Try out meeting-planning tools like the one at www.Doodle.com. Doodle is a free (or, for premium upgrade, paid) service that allows you to send suggested times to groups of people. Those who receive the request select times that work best for them. These posted times are seen by you and everyone else. You pick the meeting date based on their responses. Everyone wins!

- Planning with lots of lead time goes a long way toward finding a suitable time for all parties. Start early.

Attendee SRDs

- Keep your publicly available calendars up-to-date.

- Set permissions regarding who can schedule your calendar time and control your destiny.

- Provide consistent places in your calendar when your peers or team members know you tend to be available for meetings. For example, if you want Jon to attend, plan the meeting for Tuesday or Thursday between 10:00 AM and 12:00 noon. He typically sets aside those times for meetings.

Get Out!

Use your calendar wisely. Block off time when you need to get work done. You can choose to be *unavailable* and thus can't be automatically scheduled for a meeting.

Want a little foreshadowing? Block off your whole Friday.

65

Warning: Problem Solving
at 8 AM and 6 PM Sucks

The human mind processes billions of bits of information every day. But just like the highway getting clogged at rush hour, your mental freeways aren't free at certain times, either.

First thing in the morning, your brain flits around, already solving problems like these: "How am I going to get the information I need to get that report finished? When's payday? My right-front tire looks low, maybe I need to check the pressure. What meetings am I supposed to be in today, and how can I get out of a couple of them?"

The end of the day can be just as bad, if not worse. "Do I have any food in the house? Am I supposed to pick up Junior from practice, or is he going over to his friend's house? Has the electric bill been paid? Do I have to do laundry for tomorrow? Did I make an appointment for little Coconut at the vet? Oh, I need to check the air pressure in the tire before I get on the highway."

Would you call a phone number when you know it's busy? Then why try to reach the minds of your audience members when you know they're already busy processing a batch of information? Better to schedule your meeting for a time *after* the first batch of info has been processed and filed and *before* the next delivery of problems is expected.

Think of it this way: Diversions between those rush hours can even be welcomed. But trying to access people in the midst of other problems will be met less enthusiastically.

Facilitator SRDs

- While you might be most effective at 8 AM, it doesn't mean everyone is!

- If you plan on having the meeting at 6 PM, make sure it includes the offer of dinner and possibly a drink (if corporate liability laws permit).

- Late meetings require extra engagement techniques, so your ability to keep it upbeat and fun will be tested more than in midafternoon.

- If you're leading a late meeting, use one of the speed meeting techniques discussed in Agenda Item 3, Part 2. Quickly finish your detailed meeting objectives and go on to the evening's entertainment plans.

- If you have bad news to share and think waiting until the close of business will make it easier, then think again. Get bad news over with early, not late.

Attendee SRDs

- If it's a late meeting, you'd darn well better go in with guns ablazin'. Be prepared to get the job done and get out. People who are tired at the end of the day tend to move and think slowly. If the meeting starts this way, then step up and move the agenda along briskly, or risk spending the night in your cubicle.

- If called to attend a meeting first thing in the morning, take a few minutes, at least, to prepare for it before leaving work the day before. Don't wait until the morning; too many variables, including heavy traffic, could prevent you from making it happen before your morning meeting.

- Spend the extra buck on the double espresso shot in your skinny caramel macchiato on the way to your morning meeting.

If it's a once-a-year late meeting and dinner-type ordeal, simply make the most of it. Get the job done effectively by going in prepared and keeping the group focused. Keep away from any topics that could be addressed at other times. They'll only prolong the agony.

Get Out!

You've already tried the *prior engagement* line for the late meeting, huh? *The kids have soccer game and I'm the coach* not working, either? Then at least explain you can be there for the start but not for the whole meeting.

If you explain you have to leave by a certain time, give yourself 5 or 10 minutes of grace time and *leave late* from that stated time. This shows your dedication and willingness to *stay late* at the meeting.

If several people are making presentations, request to be first on the agenda. After your presentation, take an extended bathroom break that concludes the next morning.

If a dinner is planned for after the meeting, it's almost always easier to get out of the meeting. Just make use of the *prior engagement* line here.

68

The Overinvitation Sucks

How many times this week have you sat in a meeting and asked yourself:

- "Why I am here?"

- "Why are members of the sales team here? This issue doesn't concern them, and they're only making it worse."

- "How does this information affect me?"

- "Why can't they just let me know what decision they make? I'm fine either way."

- "What else could I be doing right now?"

- And here's the biggie: "How many times have I felt this way today?"

The *overinvitation syndrome* prevails in meeting scenarios in which the organizer has an ego problem, doesn't understand the resources needed for decision making, or doesn't want to hurt someone's feelings for *not being included*. The result? Inviting too many people to the meeting—people who may not be stakeholders in the decision, who may not need to be privy to the information, or who may not even be affected by the outcome.

Who to invite becomes a bigger decision than many might think. To alleviate the stress of deciding, meeting planners err on the side of inviting *everyone*. Unfortunately, that is counterproductive to the meeting's goals, especially if it's a problem-solving meeting. Why? **Because as you increase the number of attendees, you *exponentially* increase your inability to reach any decision.** Hence, you have a greater chance of accomplishing nothing and a bigger chance that your meeting will *suck*.

69

What about all-hands meetings, you ask? Sure, they include everyone, which is just fine as long as the organizer has studied Agenda Item 7, "Big Meetings Suck Even Bigger." Having this kind of meeting can be extremely important when the overall group is small. But as the audience size grows, so does your risk of wasting time.

In your all-hands meeting, make sure you:

- Share information that's relevant to all people. If you take a moment to speak specifically to one group, do so tactfully and broadly. A specific solution or highly detailed piece of content should be handled with group members one-on-one.

- Control the question-and-answer segment. Don't subdue the audience or dodge a tough question, but answer it as it relates to everyone by keeping focused on the group as a whole. Again, highly detailed answers relevant to a small group of attendees should absolutely be addressed—immediately after this meeting—in a direct and personal fashion.

- If all groups have the opportunity to report, keep it short, focused, and positive on how it affects the company as a whole. This shows support, builds commitment, and motivates people to do a good job.

For your everyday general meetings, determine who has a *vested interest* in reaching common objectives as opposed to who is an *interested party*. The following SRDs should help.

Facilitator SRDs

- The greater the number of people in your meeting equals the greater level of difficulty in making a decision.

- Inexperienced meeting hosts tend to overinvite. If you're one of those hosts, trim your list by asking these questions:

  - Who has the authority to make decisions on this topic?

  - Who is directly affected by the results of this decision?

  - Who will actively generate new ideas or solutions that are topical?

  - Who will contribute to the meeting in a productive manner?

  - Who has information needed for the discussion? (Attendees will become frustrated when issues can't be resolved because a key person isn't there.)

- Then consider how you'll handle the information:

  - Who needs to hear about the decision?

  - Who is affected by the results of this decision?

  - Who has a team member or team leader already participating in the meeting?

- If you want everyone holding hands in unison, invite all those who are sympathetic to the same cause. But if you want a lively discussion, then invite people on both sides of the issue at hand.

- You can still gather the view of the full group. Provide an opportunity to participate before the meeting by having people share their ideas or strategies with their team leader or liaison who will attend.

- Having secret meetings or withholding information that should be public will definitely be viewed as negative. Always share appropriate information

71

or decisions with your team and/or company leaders.

- Check your ego at the door. Your all-hands meeting must relate to *all* hands. If you're showing off your power (or need thereof) by having a mandatory meeting that isn't relevant to everyone, you're fostering dissatisfaction for your most productive workers. But don't worry; those who aren't highly productive will welcome the interruption and applaud you with all *their* hands.

Attendee SRDs

Is it not the type of meeting you can publicly back out of? Do you have an egocentric meeting leader who will be offended if you don't show up? Do you fear others will also be no-shows and thus hurt your career? Or simply, do you feel an obligation to attend knowing you'll behave like a wallflower. Consider these suggestions:

- Get involved by making the meeting relate to your objectives or your team. The facilitator may even ask you to step down from your soapbox. In that case, you simply ask, "Then may I leave?"

- Ask where the notes will be posted afterward. Then find other things to do to remain productive without further delaying the proceedings of the meeting.

- Ask a direct question: "How do the 2014 projected corn-trucking needs relate to the swimming pool maintenance department?"

Get Out!

An all-hands meeting is likely the type you need to get out of before it even starts. Ask yourself these questions:

- Do you believe you've been automatically added to a meeting invitation because you're part of a group? Then respond by saying that your supervisor or team leader will represent your team. Or, if necessary, change up and have a different representative attend each meeting. Keep as many team members productive as possible.

- TiVo the meeting. Many all-hands meetings for large companies are recorded in some fashion. If you need the information that's presented there, get the recording. That way, you can play it back without all the "commercials" (in the form of tangents, bad transitions, and useless babble).

- Have your tried these handy excuses lately? "Sorry, I have food poisoning." "I have a court date with my ex-spouse." "I'm having lunch with my mother-in-law."

Starting Late Sucks

Let me guess . . . starting late is an everyday occurrence experienced by your team—and by most of the civilized world.

9:57 AM

Chris walks by the conference room with its low table, comfy chairs, and cool pictures to see whether anyone has arrived for the project meeting. Nope, lights are still off. Plenty of time to put together his report. It's the same report as last time, anyway.

(*continued*)

9:58 AM

Lauren checks his e-mail to look for a cancellation notice for the project meeting. Rebecca walks into the conference room—the first one—and turns on the lights.

10:00 AM

Announced starting time for the meeting.

John texts Nancy. "Hey, this meeting still on?" She responds, "I think so. Going?"

10:02 AM

Deb, the host, arrives, and as she gets out the bagels and opens the cream cheese, she greets Rebecca.

10:03 AM

Mary pokes her head in to grab a bagel with a quick schmear of cream cheese. Out she goes, saying she doesn't have her notes, but she did get the lone blueberry bagel before Gene did.

10:05 AM

Jeff, Heather, and Gene arrive and head toward the bagels, laughing as they watch a YouTube clip on Gene's iPhone.

Rebecca sighs. She looks at her watch, eagerly anticipating the return to her office to finish her "real job" for the day.

10:06 AM

Chris, with his newly created report, strolls in the door. A few others follow.

10:07 AM

Small talk about last night's game can be heard around the bagel table.

10:10 AM

Deb eventually says, "Everyone, we're getting started." Low and behold—the meeting actually starts.

10:15 AM

Door opens. "I was stuck on a conference call," says George as he hurries in. "What did I miss?"

You've Been There!

Tell me this scenario isn't an everyday, *every hour* occurrence. The ever-present challenge of late meetings is one of my favorite challenges to talk about—not because I'm opposed to starting a meeting at 10 minutes past the hour or because of the social interaction and side talk. In fact, I strongly support the camaraderie that's critical to form and foster before, during, and after meetings. But I've always been among those who arrived on time and didn't have time to waste. I was prepared to walk out of the conference room and simply return when the meeting actually started.

Let me explain why this challenge has become one of my favorites.

Years ago, I was seated in a now-infamous meeting in our company's Cincinnati office. I was the guy assigned to build the sales team for my employer. I had only two people on my existing team and needed to circle the wagons to set our upcoming goals for the year.

I set an important team meeting that was scheduled to begin at 10:00 AM. I had rented a conference room and was setting it up by 9:45. I was ready to go by 9:50 and 9:55 and 9:58 and 9:59. In that final minute, I had a decision to make—one that possibly changed my path in life. What if I set the expectations for this team meeting going forward? What if I started the meeting on time—*all by myself*?

Well, that's exactly what I did. I started talking, all by myself. This was before the days of Bluetooth. (Since then, people seemingly talking to themselves

(continued)

(continued)

has become a common occurrence.) Rather, this took place in the age of people saying, "Some weird man is talking to nobody in the conference room."

About 10:06, Linda and her cohort Sally strolled into the conference room with their coffee. They took notice of me but certainly didn't worry about my presence. At least *not* until I pointed to their agendas laid out before them. I whispered, "We're on item three." That's when the jaw dropping occurred.

"We thought you were on a conference call!? Who are you talking to?" Linda said.

I didn't respond. I simply continued with the meeting.

Yeah, you can call me crazy, but guess what happened for the rest of the meetings I held with that team? People showed up *on time*. First, because they knew I'd start with or without them, and second, as the team grew, so did this story. They were afraid to find out what I'd do next!

The amount of time wasted by meetings not starting and ending on time would be astronomical if we could physically calculate it. Or maybe we can. You can go to www.BoringMeetingsSuck.com to download a simple tool that helps you calculate the *actual* cost of your meetings. Check out some apps available for your smart phone and calculate the loss in real time— perhaps during a boring meeting while planning your strategy to exit.

While the meeting host can sometimes be blamed for not starting on time, the larger problem typically lies with attendees. They routinely show up late because they expect the meeting won't formally start until 10 minutes past the hour. Why waste time being there at the designated starting time, right? Well, if the Bore No More! movement catches on in your office, you'll feel differently when your meeting host starts playing by different rules. Here are some of my most-often-used concepts that *effectively* get people to show up on time and get meetings started as planned.

Facilitator SRDs

- Just start it! If you want to take the direct path, start on time *no matter what*! Even if the president of the company is late, start anyway. He or she will respect the fact that you made good use of that time. And no offense to your meeting, but the prez just might not show up at all.

- The 11:01 principle. Schedule your meetings at an odd time, such as 11:01 or 11:31 instead of 11:00 or 11:30. It will cause people to look twice at the invitation and wonder why you'd set up something different like this. Whenever you do this, make sure you start on that minute exactly—no exceptions.

Note on first two SRDs: These work best when you're starting a new series of meetings or when you have a new team. If you try this with an existing group or ongoing meetings, I highly suggest using it in conjunction with the "social time" and "pass the pad" directives that follow.

If you start a new group using this philosophy, you've struck gold!

- *Social time.* As mentioned, meetings are definitely a time for social interaction among team members who might not have an opportunity to interact regularly. How can you foster that team growth? Give them social time! Literally schedule it in. In the meeting invitation, note the start time as 10:50 AM for bagels, conversation, and networking, with the meeting proper beginning at 11:01 AM *sharp.* Again, don't let up on this; if you say you'll start at 11:01, do it, no matter what. If people are late, "pass the pad" will take care of that. You'll quickly make many people happy to come to your meetings, and you allow the Rebecca's of the world to show up on time and get in and get out.

- *Pass the pad.* Here's an incentive to be on time: Request that notes be taken by the last person to arrive. The notes, action items, and summary must be completed by that person and posted/shared within one hour of the meeting to a server or shared platform. Likely, you'll have that favorite yellow legal pad shifted from one person to another as latecomers arrive and previous note takers heave a sigh of relief. Bonus: In addition to the incentive to arrive on time, this allows the last person who comes in to read what he or she missed.

- Close the meeting room doors at the exact start time of the meeting.

- Give the work to those who don't show up. This is my friend Bob's favorite SRD. He says the most important church service he attends regularly is on the second Sunday in June. A major holiday? No. The second Sunday in June is when Sunday school teachers are "elected" for the upcoming year. Those who don't show, get elected.

- Contribute to the coffee or bagel fund. If you show up late, you add a dollar to the jar (unless you informed the meeting host ahead of time that you'd be late).

- Always arrive early. What a concept! People don't need to see you set up your laptop and display device. Have it ready when they come in, and you'll set the tone of the meeting.

Attendee SRDs

- If the facilitator doesn't start on time or doesn't even show up on time, start the meeting on your own with those in attendance—especially if it's a regular meeting and you know the attendees and format well. Be ready to step back when the meeting host shows up and share what's happened so far.

- Be on time. If you're the culprit walking through the door after it's been closed, then stop doing this! Why not schedule in the minutes it takes to get there, including your stop-at-the-bathroom-and-wash-your-hands time. Combine this with the previous SRD and watch how the groove changes.

Get Out!

If you are the first one in the meeting room and no one else has arrived, leave your business card with a handwritten note that says something like, "I was here for the 1:00 meeting, but no one else was, so I assume it's been canceled. Call or text if the meeting still happens." Then leave a time stamp (e.g., 1:05 PM) to show you waited a few minutes. You can also write this on a paper chart, whiteboard, chalkboard, or whatever is available. When the rest of the people show up, they'll either call or text you. If they don't, then *you* win!
(*continued*)

(continued)

If everyone *has* to be in attendance before your meeting can begin, then decide right away to reschedule if a team member will be significantly delayed. It's like daylight savings time without turning the clocks back. Don't waste anyone's time if nothing can be accomplished without key people in attendance.

"Dogs Who Get Off the Leash" Suck

Will people ever stop coming up with tangents to disrupt your meeting? Let's think about that one . . . hmm, *no!*

How many times have you sat in a meeting designated for a particular purpose and out of left field flies a comment, concern, or suggestion that occupies a great portion of that meeting going forward? What's worse, the tangent creator (who may well offer a valid point) might feel the need to explain, discuss, and develop a solution right then and there. It could even involve a group of attendees who have little or nothing to do with that issue. Do these tangent creators realize they just want to hear themselves talk, or are they looking for a way to add superficial importance to their value to the organization?

When a dog gets off its leash like this, what happens? As an attendee, you look at your watch, start complaining about time being wasted, and think about the project you need to finish before the end of the day. As a facilitator, you watch as time ticks away, and you witness the rapidly diminishing engagement of your uninvolved attendees.

As the facilitator, please respect the time constraints of the attendees you've invited *and* make sure you accomplish the objectives set out in your agenda. **If the tangential**

"dog-off-the-leash" idea is critical to your discussion and a _stopper_ for moving forward, break off the meeting for those not involved. Let them get back to what they need to do. Then reconvene in a stated amount of time after a specific group has taken this tangent to the point where it plays into the initial agenda.

If you routinely have attendees who put noncritical tangents into play, and that dog keeps flying off the leash, set the example by yanking back on the chain. Do it quickly and directly to effectively ward off future challenges.

If you're a facilitator, it's important to not put down the attendees who present the tangents or make them feel like outcasts in any way. Their input could be extremely valid and valuable if it's an issue that must be addressed.

Do this: Accept their ideas and empower them to develop solutions before occupying the precious time of non-involved attendees. You'd say, "That's a great idea, Vern, and we need to look at that. Why don't you put together your thoughts and data on this, and we'll review them after this meeting."

A bigger question is how will you, if you're a mere attendee of said meeting, teach the "heel" command? By stepping up and taking action. As part of the Bore No More! movement, you have equal rights and responsibilities to make meetings more effective. If you sit back and allow Left-Field Leroy to take the meeting off track, then you've forfeited your right to complain.

Whatever position you're in, you'd better learn quickly. If you don't, you're out for a _long_ walk instead of a boring meeting. Bring along the plastic baggie for the crap that will result.

81

Facilitator SRDs

- Establish a "parking lot" for ideas that need to be addressed but aren't appropriate for this meeting or this group. If your meetings are prone to time-wasting tangents, this can be a great way to side-step them while still accepting them as valuable. Do this by establishing a predefined "parking lot" chart or area of the whiteboard. When off-subject items come up, "park them" by writing them in this special area so those who've spoken up feel appeased. Then assign a person and/or date for following up on these issues.

- If you don't like having meetings that are do-overs (see "Déjà Meetings Suck" under Agenda Item 6), then you'd better make sure you come back to these parking lot items eventually.

- If you're expecting a person to bring up something you know is *not* relevant, address it with that person ahead of time in a professional way. Either discuss it personally before the meeting or set up a separate time to review it afterward.

- Establish a "cop" for each meeting, a person to police the group to stay on task. Make sure you change personnel often, though, so the task doesn't go to their egos to start policing all the functions in the office. You're not looking for "Dwight" from NBC-TV's *The Office*!

Attendee SRDs

- Your meeting leader's ability to recognize a tangent and redirect it may be lacking. Don't be afraid to suggest items go to the parking lot or to tell Left-Field Leroy that the primary topics need to be addressed first.

82

- Hold up your agenda and point to the item you're supposed to be addressing. Or point to the clock or your watch. No dialogue necessary.

- Tell the facilitator to schedule a meeting on that topic after finishing this meeting's objectives.

- Bring plenty of other work to do, so at least you can get something done today.

Get Out!

If the tangent appears to be a stopper for your originally planned agenda or objectives, and you have no involvement in those objectives, you need to get out. Combine politeness and assertiveness to serve your greater purpose. You can:

- Address the meeting facilitator, boss, or person who had the initial objectives and ask if you should begin working on those objectives separately with a group, or simply ask, "Will we reschedule?" Give that person an either/or question; you know that staying in this cage is *not* an option.

- Ask the facilitator whether you'll still cover today's intended objectives and ask what time should you be back. If those items won't be covered, that's fine. You just need know so you can finish other work related to this group.

It's possible that addressing your concerns this way will trigger the meeting to get back on track. Of course, you could also wait it out and not complain, but that's no fun—and not the purpose of this agenda item.

83

Conference Rooms Suck

We've looked at why and how we meet, but what about where?

When was the last time you thought about the physical location or attributes of your meeting space? Was it extra space that a conference table and whiteboard could fit in without much thought? Is your conference room a place where old chairs and furniture go before they die? When attendees enter a 1970s crusty, wallpapered, stinky room (you know the one I mean), how does it make them feel?

Attendees or even facilitators don't commonly think about these aspects of a meeting room, but they should. Let's consider what you might do, and heed advice from a few experts as well.

In a recent blog post I asked, "Where have your best and worst meetings taken place?" Here are just a few of my favorite responses. Pick which ones are yours.

- Disney.

- A morgue.

- A cubicle in a warehouse where countless items were being shipped during the holiday season.

- Conference room overlooking Times Square in NYC.

- Movie theater, complete with popcorn and snacks.

- An 8' × 12' conference room with a 7' × 11' table. No windows, floor-to-ceiling whiteboard on every wall, and too many florescent lights. It felt like an interrogation room from a (very) low-budget cop movie. Oh, and it was in New Jersey.

Worst-Case Scenario

My toughest conference room environment in which I was presenting was the Breakers Hotel in West Palm Beach, Florida—about 20 attendees in total with 10 on either side of a huge table. The 10 on the opposite side of where I stood wouldn't have known if a brick hit them. While half the people looked across the table at them, they could stare out the windows and see the beach. And right in front of the window was a path where beachgoers walked back and forth wearing *skimpy beach attire.*

Chalk that up as Jon Petz = 0, Beach = 1.

Some of these examples are far out, and didn't come cheap, but here's the point. Your meeting doesn't have to take place in a room with a long table and chairs. The instant your team members walk into that room, they might instinctively want to settle in and become brain dead. Why? Because that's what they've always done in this room.

Besides the well-worn groove in the carpet that acts as the guiding light to your conference room, do you always need to have your meetings there? In fact, do you even need to call it a conference room? The very word *conference* doesn't energize 'em. How about you? Because most meetings are collaborative in nature, let's go with *collaboration room*, or better yet, let's learn more about what's known as *collaboration space.*

Mark Henson, founder and chief imagination officer of Sparkspace, offers great advice on creating better conference space. Meeting planners from around the country have visited his facility in Columbus, Ohio, to see what he does so well.

85

Sparkspace is a one-of-a-kind conference, teamwork, and personal development center where it's impossible to have an ordinary, boring business meeting. From the overstuffed chairs, full-wall working spaces, and interactive nature of each specialized room, it's been designed and built from the ground up to provide space built around collaboration and inspiration.

> **Mark says that the majority of conference rooms are built with efficiency in mind instead of group interaction and dynamics.**

So rather than build three rooms designed to be all things to all people, why not look at specific functions for each room, with carryover effects? No need to have a kitchen table in every room of the house, is there? Think lots of variety.

Many meeting rooms are also being "overtechnified," which means technology is put into place without the participants understanding why they should use it or even how to do so. I've been to many a venue or conference center with the fancy tech-savvy podiums or devices, but the only people who can get those devices to work are the audio-visual specialists on-site. Breaking up your meeting to call in the AV guy isn't what you had in mind when you planned your meeting, was it? It breaks into the whole "attendee engagement" thing you're striving for. Don't abuse the technology just because the designer/builder says you need the next cool thing in the marketplace.

Brandon Dupler, the principal at Dupler Office, specializes in creating places that enable and inspire workers to achieve their best. He believes that the right design of an office space can inspire performance, enhance productivity, increase morale, and create exceptional value. The key word I hear from Brandon, many times over is *space,* not *room.*

86

"Take down the walls and get rid of the table," Brandon says. "Seating should be comfortable, flexible, and mobile so meeting hosts can arrange the space however they want for optimal interaction based on their goals. As personal space continues to shrink, people need their collaborative space to increase—space in which they can interact with each other and with their technology seamlessly. If they can't, the space is useless."

In place of a standard break room, perhaps you could create a café with a mix of high-top tables, wooden stools, lounge seating, coffee tables, and fast, secure wireless connectivity. Which do you think would be used more? And why not set up a collaboration space among sections of cubicles for quick meet-and-greet sessions with your team?

If you want to build or rent some of the greatest meeting space imaginable, Mark and Brandon are two people you'll want to meet. But what about all the not-so-hip folks who have only a conference room and no time or budget to build a new one? Here are suggestions for what you *can* do.

Facilitator SRDs

Get out of the stinkin' box:

- Do you even need to use a conference room? What about your local or state park—or even an amusement park? Trust me, a few times on one of those "spinning thingies" can generate wild ideas. Hit the swings and then talk about your plans imaginatively. You'll find that exercise gets the blood flowing to the brain far better than an ergonomic chair.

- Don't think your boss will go for the park idea? What about the building lobby, rooftop, coffee shop, or local library to break the norm? The key is not to skip class but to prove your ability to get the job done in an environment that fosters collaboration instead of enduring the dullness of a conference room.

- Pick a place that has wireless or 3G/4G access or better.

Stuck with your box? Do this:

- Lose the table. How can you create a "new space" feel in your existing space?

- Invest in furniture that people want to sit in. Are the seats mobile so you can move them around your collaboration space?

- Fluorescent lights suck. Anytime you can bring in sunlight without blinding people, do it! If you're in interior building space, bring in additional lamps or lighting that uses natural-lighting-type lightbulbs, and turn off those overhead tubes of turmoil.

- Whether inside four walls or in an open environment, fast connectivity is critical. If people have to share, you don't want that slowing them down—including that LCD panel or screen on the wall that users can connect to wirelessly. Look for off-the-shelf solutions that offer easy Bluetooth or network connectivity to these screens. Use them! (Most laptops even come with it.)

- Bring in power plugs and strips; you can't have enough.

- Set up easy access to refreshments that are brain healthy; skip the typical junk food.

- Unless you're a family legal firm, take photos of old people off the walls. Yeah, motivational or team-work art pieces can be nice, but you need to change

88

them often. Otherwise, they become just like those "lose weight" reminders on the fridge, simply blending in like bacon after you've seen them a dozen times. Better yet, get the *Boring Meetings Suck* calendar or posters at www.BoringMeetingsSuck.com. Now you're thinking!

- In appropriate weather, open the windows and enjoy the fresh air.

- When you can, keep the door of the room open (unless you're making a point about starting on time to the latecomers). A closed door makes many people feel trapped, and it may block out natural light from a window or other doorway.

- Have a lot of extra chairs? Take time to move them to the side or out of the room.

- How does the room smell? Place in the room a small bowl of potpourri or a candle that smells like peppermint or chocolate to stimulate the brain. A quick shot of air freshener can work wonders as well. Remember walking into a room after a horrid case of BO lingered from the people before you? You don't want to replicate that lackluster experience.

- *Nobody* likes sitting at a dirty conference table that has crusted cream cheese left over from the last group. Take time to wipe it off, and disinfect the table if you plan to have food.

- Keep in mind that space you use for an internal meeting doesn't have to be the same room you use for a client meeting. The client meeting room could have a more formal feel for sales presentations, while the internal one might be more functional for internal team and collaboration-type meetings.

89

- Arrive at the room first and arrange it in the ways already noted. If the meeting host doesn't do any of this, you can.

- Door closed? No reason? Take a bathroom break or step out to take a call and leave the door open when you step back in.

- If Rocking Robyn sits next to you and won't stop bouncing back and forth (can you say *annoying*?), reach over and lock the chair recline lever. No need to say anything. Or you could coax her to get a chair that doesn't rock.

Mark Henson (www.Sparkspace.com) adds these suggestions:

What every conference room should have: Space to move. If your conference room is 8′ × 10′ and your conference table is 7′ × 9′, there is something seriously wrong with the table-size-to-room-size ratio. Sometimes the best ideas come when we get up and change our perspective.

What conference rooms should never have: Photos of the founders of the company or pictures of ships on a stormy ocean. I've seen both in conference rooms and they're *creepy.* Dogs playing poker would be acceptable, though.

Brandon Dupler (www.DuplerOffice.com) offers these ideas:

What every conference should have: Great chairs and great refreshments.

What conference rooms should never have: One of those old podiums where the speaker is built into the front of it, and you have to deal with that long, silver, bendy microphone holder that makes a horrendous sound when you move it.

Get Out!

Arrive at the conference room early to nab the seat by the door for your planned exit strategy. At least you're in a position to see the people on the outside, and they can pass you signs of encouragement. If the room does smell, the nausea excuse works, too. No one wants to see you hurl while you huddle.

Meetings are inevitable. Because they're so prevalent, anyone and everyone involved in any kind of meeting needs to help plan and execute whatever meeting is at hand—including the after-meeting activities. Once *everyone* takes responsibility, then the meeting can actually accomplish what it's supposed to!

Agenda Item 5

Your Presentation
Sucks . . . Really, *Yours* Sucks

Hey, while this item may look like it's for presenters only, look again.

As a meeting attendee, you can assist your meeting facilitator by reading the ideas here. Plus, who knows? One day you might be front and center, under the hot lights of the projector, desperately needing to make your presentation more effective. Ignore my suggestions at your peril (insert your own evil-sounding laugh here)!

First, a few questions for you as a presenter:

What makes meetings and presentations effective? *You.*
What makes meetings and presentations suck? *You.*
So, what's the difference (besides you)?

It's your *ability to effectively engage people* in the content you're delivering. It's having your attendees desire to listen, participate, and interact to achieve the outcomes you desire from your meeting.

That's a lot to ask? Sure it is, especially when Monotone Mitch steps up to read five PowerPoint slides packed with 27 bullet points about why this meeting is imperative.

93

Meetings require someone to lead them. I've been calling that person a meeting *facilitator,* but, really, facilitators are much more: the teacher and the referee, the person in charge of handling the unruly students (. . . oops, I mean fellow attendees and team members) in the back.

Attendees expect their meeting leader to be an interesting presenter and to engage them creatively, intellectually, or both, depending on the kind of meeting.

> **Attendees quickly become disgruntled if the
> meeting goes off track, and they
> don't want to feel chained to their
> conference-room chairs.**

As a presenter, you don't want people to get up and leave. There's a lot at stake here.

Repeatedly, it's been proven that those who can present themselves effectively in front of an audience can better influence thoughts, build consensus, and recruit followers to join them on their missions. Just look at our wonderful elected politicians (yes, please read sarcasm into that statement). If you're in that camp, great. Or possibly you are like the vast majority of people who would rather die than have to present in public.

As I said in the Introduction, meetings are presentations, in part. By definition, *presentations* consist both of the person standing up and talking to a group and the materials the presenter uses.

If you think of presentations as an art form, it implies there's no systematic way of telling you what's good and what's not. In fact, this subject could take up an entire book (which I won't shamelessly promote because I

94

haven't written it yet!). But for the purposes of *this* book, let me share important pointers about how to be a better presenter to avoid a boring and ineffective meeting. This not only includes how to engage your audience, but also how to use PowerPoint, how to avoid hmms and ums, how to keep from droning on, and more.

To do that, let's revisit your first speech class for a minute (if you ever had one). You learned that the most important elements of a speech—you know, the ones you got graded on—were eye contact, great visual aides, powerful stories to back up your point, and not going over your time limit.

> **Not only is this the all-you-need-to-know-is-everything-you-learned-in-speech-class part of the book, but it focuses on the most critical tool in any meeting presenter's toolbox:** *how to engage an audience.*

If you're presenting at a meeting, you are partly engaged in, dare I say it, *public speaking.* After all, you're in front of a group of people, and you're speaking, so hence, you're speaking publicly. Scary thought, isn't it?

Yet think of public speaking as an extension of your speech class, an art form that engages the senses of those in the audience and stirs them into new ways of thinking.

> *Good* **public speaking invites active participation, encouraging everyone to make new mental connections.** *Great* **public speaking features creative dialogue that inspires change.**

If you participated on the debate team or took part in school plays or musicals, you're at an advantage when you

95

get in front of people today. These fabulous experiences taught you how to communicate in a group. But if you didn't do these activities in high school, don't despair. Help is on the way. Just take a deep breath and keep reading.

If you're charged with running a meeting, you may think being a good or even a great presenter is a lot to ask. I also realize you likely haven't taken classes on how to be engaging. Sure, you can find fabulous publications on how to be social and interact well with others. You can even find books on engagement practices in the workplace. No doubt your city's "free university" offers classes on how to create an experience for your audience. But finding a class on how to *effectively and emotionally* engage a five-person audience—with or without PowerPoint slides? Don't bank on it.

I've worked with a ton of people, many of whom fit in the camp of "deathly afraid of public speaking." I'm fortunate enough to be one of the few who drools at the opportunity to speak in public. Actually, I did start out as a shy child, but I eventually developed a high level of comfort in front of a group. And you can, too.

When I work with people who want to become better presenters and facilitators, I find it's important not to push them to change their personalities or who they are as people. Instead, I find ways to help them feel comfortable by offering new presentation tips or ideas that grab the attention of attendees . . . and keep it!

Although I can't teach you how to be the best presenter in the world in the next few pages, I can encourage you by saying this: *In your presentation, the key is to convey information in a way that creates the most impact for your intended purpose.*

To make sure speeches and presentations don't suck, the first subjects I address when working with individuals, sales teams, and speakers are:

- PowerPoint Sucks

- "Um . . . aah" Sucks

- PowerPoint *Really* Sucks

- Monotone Speeches and Movements Suck

- Unreadable Slides Suck

- Cutesy Moving Graphics Suck

Let's discuss them one by one.

PowerPoint Sucks

Would you like me to shout it? *PowerPoint sucks*!

If you've ever attended a meeting of any sort, and I mean *any* sort, you could no doubt instantly identify with the conclusion in this heading.

This well-known and widely blamed software tool from Microsoft Corporation makes it easy to create, manage, and share presentations in person, on a mobile device, or via the Internet. This software represents the single greatest abuse when it comes to making meetings *suck*—even the most updated version.

Let's begin with the most important principle of this abuse—providing graphic representations to back up your facts and figures. Yes, PowerPoint delivers visual and audio stimuli that build emotion and engagement into the subject you're presenting. But remember, its purpose is to *enhance*

97

your presentation . . . at least that's what I wish the instruction manual said!

However, the vast majority of people use PowerPoint (or an equivalent, such as Keynote for Mac computers) *as the presentation itself.* What happened to using visuals to *enhance* your own presentation, not as a substitute for it? That's why we can't blame PowerPoint outright. When your PowerPoint slides suck, you have only *you* to blame—you and your unknown desire to deliver mindless presentations when you could simply have shared the presentation via other means.

> **I will say it boldly. PowerPoint is an effective tool when used properly. It can never be a substitute for an engaging message. That comes from you. If your presentation relies entirely on PowerPoint, then your presentation sucks.**

But hey, don't think I'm alone in believing this. Countless blogs, books, and articles discussing presentation-type software contend that PowerPoint and its brethren reduce meetings to a compilation of poorly executed bullet points with small text and flying graphics.

The fact is, the moment you dim the lights and your attendees start getting pummeled with slides, they naturally go into lecture mode, thus reducing your meeting to a one-way, noninteractive experience.

PowerPoint has been so long abused that it destructively sucks all the energy out of your meeting. You can compound the problem by turning your shoulder and facing toward the screen as you read slide after slide in a color scheme that's difficult to view. If that's what you do, you've just doomed your meeting. Consider your attendees down for the count.

With a massive amount of material written on the subject and a vast resource of information on the Internet, let's keep this diatribe brief. That said, if you *must* use Power-Point, here are some SRDs that will put you miles ahead of other presenters. Use them and launch the Bore No More! movement in your office. It's easy.

Want more detailed information? Visit the *Boring Meetings Suck* web site and be on the lookout for *PowerPoint Sucks, the Sequel,* as well as the made-for-TV movie.

Presenter SRDs

- The PowerPoint is *not* the presentation; you are! Learn it; live it!

- The vastness of your slide arsenal has no bearing on your ability to communicate effectively. If your slides are text-heavy and unfocused, then expect results like this:

Number of slides	Result of showing them
1–15	Potential for an effective presentation if used only as visual support.
16–24	Too many. You're losing your audience.
25–34	If content-heavy and text-based, thanks for coming!
35+	Please accept our free gift: *PowerPoint Sucks*.

The purpose of this list? To tell you to keep the Power-Point part of your presentation as short as possible. Fewer slides with fewer points per slide help attendees stay focused on you and more engaged.

- *Open your pitch with something more engaging then dimming the lights.* Do you really need a title slide when you begin? Don't these people know you anyway? Instead, refer to the projected slides only when you need to or when your content dictates it.

- *Keep the lights on.* If your image doesn't show up, get a better projector. If this isn't an option, dim the lights only during the phases requiring low lighting and then turn them back up for more content and your conclusion. Worst case, it wakes up the people you've put to sleep.

- *Don't dim the lights at all.* Stop using a projector and get an LCD display viewable by everyone in your meeting space. Then you don't have to worry about silhouettes or that bright beam of light burning your retinas.

- *It's okay not to have anything on the screen.* Don't feel you have to have a slide, photo, or graphic on the screen at all times. If you want the screen to go dark or have a slide go away completely when you are finished, press *b* on your keyboard. The screen will instantly turn off (go black) and quickly turn back on when you press *b* again. If you prefer, the screen can go white by using the *w* key (who said they weren't clever over there at Gates's Microsoft complex?)

- *Insert a black or white slide.* If you're working with a remote control and don't have access to the keyboard, insert a slide that's all black or all white wherever needed in your presentation when you want all the focus on you. (I recommend black so you can then walk in front of the projector without causing

100

shadows.) Amazingly, some remotes have a special button built in with a blackout function.

- *Do you use your slides as your outline?* If you have to have slides to guide you along, then create two presentations. Develop the first one with all the text and commentary you wish to present. This version doubles as your handout or follow-up documentation. Then go back and create the actual PowerPoint you'll use in the meeting. Take out all except the most important points. The SRDs that follow will help you create your presentation slides, so keep reading.

- *Do you really have to push the button?* Do you walk over and press a button on the laptop to advance the slide, or say to someone, "Next slide, please"? Really? Seriously? Get a remote to advance your slides so you can walk around. Better yet, use the timer function that automatically advances the slides after a specified amount of seconds or minutes. Not only is it seamless, but it keeps those "dogs off the leash" at a distance. If you are in desperate need to stop the show, it's easy to pause by using the *s* key on the keyboard and pressing it again to resume. *Use bullet points in place of full sentences.* However, too many bullet points on a single slide can detract. I favor using additional slides in place of putting too much text on one slide, even in the form of bullet points— a maximum of five.

- *Maintain eye contact.* If nothing else, learn to make your primary points while engaging your audience visually. Walk away from the lectern and interact with attendees. Have at least three main points to summarize that don't require reading from the screen.

- *With and without the slides, be sure to enunciate and pronounce your words clearly.*

101

In the end, do your homework. If you're making a large or important presentation, take time to rehearse the media you'll use. Practice controlling your PowerPoint program so it fits with your complete presentation. Know when you need to advance the slides and how each relates to the content you're talking about.

Beware. If you intend to use PowerPoint or a similar program, be prepared for an instinctive reaction of boredom. It's nothing against you, just something that your ancestors have bred into humankind.

"Um . . . aah" Sucks

"*Aah*, and here, as you can see, *um* . . . is the, *aah*, same diagram but with the, *aah*, added cost of, *um*, advertising. And, *aah* . . . if we continue to grow this group then, *um*, we, *aah*, need to control this expense."

Put me down now! I can't take it. You are boring people to death at 60 *aah*s per minute. Wanna lose your audience's attention quickly and make sure your meetings suck even more? Then just, *aah*, keep *aah*, *um*, doing this, and you'll be guaranteed to succeed.

While a few of these *aah* and *um* speech habits are common and have meaning beyond revealing a speaker's discomfort, a multitude of them can drastically affect your ability to keep audiences engaged in your presentation.

What are they? Linguists call them *neutral vowel sounds*, and they're said to be the easiest sounds to make in the English language. Yup, that means other languages have different sayings: In other languages, you may hear "*eh*," (Spanish) or "*etto*" (Japanese). You may also hear in English phrases such as "you know" or "like" inserted into speech.

102

People use *um* or *aah* in conversation when they anticipate a delay and want to avoid a silent gap in speech that could be confusing to a listener. Similarly, a presenter might emit a growl-like *uh* or *aah* sound to avoid that confusing moment of silence. The problem occurs when these stall tactics take on lives of their own and not one single sentence can be uttered without an *um*, *uh*, or *aah*. Attendees not only see you as continually searching for words, but you also risk losing your credibility as the expert on your topic. High stakes.

Many years ago, I was hired by a certain college to speak to high school seniors about the benefits of higher education in general and on that college in particular. Some weeks, I'd spend on as many as four days speaking, doing as many as eight 45-minute presentations *a day*!

During the training for that program, I'd listen to the other speakers and they'd listen to me rehearse our fully scripted presentation. More important, we were asked to note every *um*, *uh*, or *aah*.

From that day forward, I have frequently given a piece of scrap paper to a presenter at the end of a meeting with data like this:

"Ums"—27
"Aahs"—41

I even include all the ticks and hash marks I made so the presenter can see how carefully I kept track of them.

I also tell the surprised speaker in a polite way that most people have no idea that they have these verbal habits; it's totally natural to them; I just want to help them for next time.

103

Do you instantly want to appear as a seasoned presenter? Fix this! You weren't born with this habit, you know. If you don't fix it, your attendees will be more distracted by the interruptions than drawn into the real content. That affects your credibility, and your effectiveness as a presenter drops through the floor.

Presenter SRDs

- Ask a trusted friend or adviser to count how many times you say *umm, uh,* or *aah* in an upcoming presentation. My bet? You'll be astonished by the high number.

- Realize that allowing a moment of silence is okay. While it feels unbelievably painful at first to be on stage and not say anything, consider it a powerful weapon. As a professional speaker and entertainer, I have learned that silence can add impact and humor while helping attendees focus on key message points. Use it wisely.

- Memorize your most important impact lines and points. Remember that you are the expert at this given moment; this is why you are presenting. Take a few minutes to rehearse your top three statements or points you want to make. Go ahead and watch in the mirror as you recite and memorize those points. *A memorized line is much less likely to include an um or aah.* Presenting an entire presentation that's obviously memorized can suck, but if you deliver your key points directly to your audience with emotion and conviction, you'll have a dramatically different result and be far more memorable and effective. When you do this, take notice of how your audience's engagement in your presentation changes—for the better—when you speak to them in this manner.

- Have a dire need to correct your actions quickly in a simple way? Trust me on this one suggestion. It works. Place a rubber band on either wrist and, for starters, keep it there for one week. Every time you say *um* or *aah*, in any dialogue, discreetly reach down and snap yourself with the rubber band. No need to draw blood here, folks, just do this as a reminder to show your subconscious mind how many times you actually use those words. You probably haven't even been aware how often you engage in this annoying habit. Doing this brings your subconscious habit to the front of your mind.

Taking a conscious approach to correcting these unconscious stalling techniques allows you to become more acutely aware of the extent of your problem. Fix it, and you'll take big steps toward driving the audience engagement you want.

PowerPoint *Really* Sucks

I couldn't possibly say enough previously, so I'm back for more.

PowerPoint is a crutch. Perhaps you use it to convey the message and lead the presentation because you're afraid to stand up and make it on your own. Remember, any slide you show should add meaning, emotion, and impact to what you are presenting.

What's the number one complaint about PowerPoint? It's boring. How do you make it not so boring? Simple. Marry your data to emotion—feelings that are universal.

Your meeting attendees have two sides of the brain and two ways of thinking: facts and figures on one side,

105

emotions on the other. It has been scientifically proven through functional MRIs and brain-based learning research that information tied to emotions has a far greater retention rate than that of bullet points listing analytical data. However, most of the billions of slides presented each year still focus heavily on the data—the facts and figures. What is there to appeal to the emotional side, to paint a mental image that people can relate to and recall?

If it's important to convey detailed facts and figures in your presentation, then do yours differently, and let your attendees sing your praises for giving them a break from the norm.

Create slides that trigger senses other than those that drive brains into a downward dive from data overload.

Involving emotions can be as simple as using image and media clips (while avoiding cutesy graphics, as you'll learn about). Yet so many people refrain from doing this, either because they lack knowledge of PowerPoint or because they think it's inappropriate. Whatever the case, in place of endless bullets of text on your slides, insert a single image—a photo, a cartoon, an illustration—that's related to the text. You've just taken charge of your presentation! Yes, you can still convey the facts and figures with the image on the screen. That way, you let the audience make the mental connection of how it applies to the business unit, team, or company. Remember, PowerPoint is there to *enhance* your presentation, not substitute for it.

Not sure how to do that? Let's address images that bring to mind an emotion or reaction—and I'm talking photos, not clip art. Check out iStock photo (www.iStock Photo.com), Getty Images (www.GettyImages.com), Big Stock (www.BigStockPhoto.com), and other royalty-free-image web sites. You'll find lots of quality images available at a reasonable cost.

How do you find what you can use? On the home page of any one of these sites, type in key words of the message you're are trying to convey, and you will be provided with a plethora of image choices.

Better yet, capture your own images from your work, industry, or community. With today's high-tech digital cameras, you can become an amateur photographer and capture the right moment with the right people, and the image makes the mental connection clearly. That allows attendees to instantly relate to your photo and thus get more out of your presentation. Feel free to keep the visuals fun and upbeat to help you Bore No More!

When you're confident about how to select photo images, step up to audio and video samples. PowerPoint now makes it easier than ever to embed media and play videos seamlessly on cue. You can stay away from the audio or video samples included with the software and add your own music, sound effects, and recordings to the presentation. Novelty works! People love new things, because they're engaging and fun. Always remember this: *People who are laughing are people who are listening*.

Want additional reading and examples of great presentations? I suggest reading Garr Reynolds's blog, at www.PresentationZen.com, for a continually updated dialogue on this topic.

- Work to reduce text, and try to implement multi-media (video and audio) into your presentation. Remember, your PowerPoint should add to your meaning or encourage additional dialogue, not become the center point for the presentation.

- You don't need to spend thousands of dollars on graphic designers and custom images when you can access millions of images online at a reasonable cost.

- Including a title or a few key words of text with a photo is great; including a whole paragraph is not.

- Share your presentation with a few peers before you present it, especially the first time. Ask whether the images or media deter from the message or create a connection with your content. If the answer is, "Yes, they add connection," then go back and determine your main point, desired outcome, or key words for each slide, and search for images or media that relate.

- All movies have soundtracks that bubble up emotions in their scenes. Why not add a little background music for effect? Is doesn't have to be serious music. Try this one: As you recap your final points and share the grand plan to move forward, play something like the theme to the classic film *Rocky*. People may giggle and you can as well, but I bet they'll remember what you said.

- Refrain from using images you don't have permission to use or audio/video material that's copyrighted and not your legal property.

- Fade (gradually lower) your audio when possible; a hard cut (abrupt change) in music sounds jerky and unprofessional. How can you soften it? Get some basic audio-editing software. You can find several options on the Internet, including Audacity (free, open-source software for recording and editing that is easy to use and works on all computing platforms).

- Be certain all images are appropriate for your audience.

- Instead of continual bullet points, insert a photograph of what those points represent. Save the majority of your bullets for the handout and your dialogue. Bullets visually dull the senses and can put a bullet through the attention span of your attendees. (I couldn't resist.)

If you want to make a quick connection with even more emotional appeal, then add media samples. If you merely want to get analytical data out to the masses, then post it to the company's server, for gosh sakes, and get on with your day.

Monotone Speeches and Movements Suck
Bueller . . . Bueller . . . Bueller?

If you're up on your 1980s classic films, you can't get by this without being taken back to the economics class in *Ferris Bueller's Day Off* (Paramount Pictures, 1986). The teacher has a class full of sleeping, drooling students bored by his tedious monotone, his ongoing babble with no inflection or vibe whatsoever. Who could blame Ferris for skipping out? Wouldn't you do everything you could to get out?

I do need to preface this part by saying I understand it's hard to get up in front of a bunch of people, especially people you know, and give a presentation. You might be nervous or scared and have a dry throat. You might just want to get it over with. What do you do? You present with a dry, unenthusiastic, monotone voice that instantly dulls even the brightest of senses that may be tuned in. To make matters worse, you read your slides and never move a muscle. You stay put behind the lectern or in your corner of the conference room and don't add a single shred of body language to your effort. God forbid you look at Sue, your cubicle mate, and see her staring at you, her eyes pleading with you to *get it over with.*

So you drone on. And on. And on.

Your voice and your body are your most valuable tools when you present, but they are also the most underused. The result? No emotion, no feeling, no eye contact, no movement, no life whatsoever—like Bueller's teacher. You are so much in the zone of drone that you don't even know whether your audience is asleep—that is, until you realize those sounds behind you are elongated snores from the audience.

> **Snoring . . . is applause for boring meetings.**

Again, I totally understand why you might be tempted to seek the shelter of the large wooden pedestal of protection in front of you and read right through your notes without once looking up. *You're nervous and anxious.* These feelings are the true enemies of a presentation, and they can cause you, the presenter, to look for a way to get off the stage in the fastest possible way.

> **A great presenter can provide mediocre information and be highly successful; a mediocre presenter can give great information and fail miserably.**

In a casual conversation, if you speak in monotone and don't move, you may have an insurmountable problem. But since I've only met *two people* like that in my entire life, I'll assume that when you talk to others in casual conversations, you're relaxed, even animated. That's exactly what you're going for in front of a group of people. I'm here to tell you that you can do this easily and effectively, but it will take practice.

You've seen celebrities and political figures on television make emphatic points in appearances or speeches. I suspect you're in awe of their natural flow, charisma, and ease in front of audiences. What no one sees are the hours upon hours of training and rehearsal that went into their presentations or appearances.

I'm not saying you need to run out and take a ton of classes on how to be a better public speaker (although one or two certainly won't hurt). But I do suggest you look at your own presentation style and understand what natural characteristics you have that can make your presentation style most effective *if you emphasize them more.*

Audiences want to relate to presenters, to connect with them. Hiding behind the lectern and speaking with no inflection doesn't help make that bond. To change this habit could be a hefty step outside your comfort zone.

Here are some tricks I teach. Use them to help bring forth the Bore No More! movement in your workplace so your organization can have fewer meetings that suck.

1. **The "Run and Drag" Technique.** If your speaking style is *all drag*, then change the tempo. With this pacing technique, you hurry up a group of words to share your excitement of them. You follow up that

111

spurt with a short pause, then deliver the next group of words at a slower, drawn-out rate. Here's an example.

Spoken at an accelerated rate: "When I asked him how he feels this could impact his bottom line and how his customers could benefit from it . . ." [*pause*]

Spoken at a slow rate: ". . . he said . . . 'I *think* I like it.'"

Do this to make a key point more forceful, to illustrate a story, or to enhance the punch line of a joke. You'll find it alters your pace of speech and keeps it lively and interesting.

2. **The Effective Pause.** It feels uncomfortable to be onstage with nothing happening. But while *nothing* is happening onstage, *something* is happening in the minds of your attendees. If you want them to think twice about what you just said, use this drama-based tip—the *pause.* I don't mean take a breath; I mean make it an actual pause to a slow count of "one, one thousand" or even more.

Why do this? Because it signals that what you've just said or are about to say is important, so listeners pay more attention. Here's an example.

Without the pause: "Today, we are going to talk about technology, texting, and using Twitter in meetings."

With several pauses: "Today, we are going to talk about
Technology . . . [short pause]
Texting . . . [short pause]
and . . . [a little longer pause] using Twitter . . . in meetings."

If you were sitting in a class taking notes, which example makes it easier and encouraging for you to write down what was just said?

112

Effectively using a pause also breaks up the monotony of any speech and gives it audible breathing space. Think of it as having white space in a printed advertisement. It's just as important to have open space on parts of the page as it is to have the writing and graphics. White space makes the words and pictures stand out more.

3. **Stories.** As a professional speaker, I know that telling stories is paramount to engaging audience members. Stories can be used to kick off or close the presentation in an entertaining way, or they can be used in the middle if they have a message that relates to your content material.

   Stories also allow you to talk from your own *voice*. It's much easier to talk in a conversational tone and share some emotion and verbal inflection when relating a funny story that happened to you. Storytelling puts you at ease, thus releases tension, which is especially important at the beginning to get you in a groove. This not only puts *you* in a happy, place but audience members, too.

   Do yourself a favor. Whenever possible, use personal stories instead of searching the Internet for them and claiming they happened to you.

4. **Humor.** Comedy doesn't come naturally to every presenter. But don't think for a minute you have to be a comedian, great joke teller, or entertainer to pull off a funny bit. Humor can be subtle, and it can be in verbal form, printed form, or visual form. Laughter not only allows the brain to revitalize with oxygen and wake up the body, it also enables listeners to go deeper in the topic they are learning about.

   Look for ways to kick off your presentation with a funny YouTube video, or play one in the middle to break up the session. Humor can help people remember who you are, illustrate a point, and create a

113

bond with your audience. It allows your audience to recognize that you are human, especially when you make fun of yourself.

Here's a funny, yet accurate, one-liner I hear all the time at my National Speakers Association professional organization meetings:

"Do I need humor in my talk?"

"Only if you want to get paid."

5. **Movement and Eye Contact.** I've said it before and I'm saying it again because it's so important. You're guaranteed a death sentence if you stand behind a lectern and never once attempt to release yourself from its safety grip. Same holds true if you never attempt to acknowledge anyone in the audience.

First, let's talk about eye contact. And I don't mean a random glance up from your notes for a mere second. Eye contact is a planned action of speaking directly with a person or a group of people. You want to address groups of people for five seconds at a time before moving on to the next group or person. Let them know you're *talking* to them, not just glancing in their direction.

Now about that lectern. Take baby steps and gradually distance yourself from its iron grip. The audience needs visual movement, even if that means stepping to either side of it at different times. You can do this and still see your notes if you need to. Once you've mastered stepping aside, you then gradually feel comfortable working the room. Your goal is to walk around and interact directly with individuals or groups.

6. **Body Language.** Body language during your presentation can be as important as your words. Your physical actions and movements can tell a story, build rapport, and share emotion. Start simply—with just a smile—and people will quickly feel more

114

comfortable with you. If you want the audience to be uncomfortable, then let them see you hiding behind the lectern, fidgeting with microphone cable, tapping pencils, or worse yet, looking down at your phone to check the Twitter feed about this meeting—how boring it is and how badly people want out!

Move, please move. Do anything except just stand in one place. If you have to make personal notes to yourself to "*move stage left*" or "*gesture here,*" then do it. Just don't read those parts out loud, okay? Presidents and political leaders are always analyzed for their gestures and hand movements, which drive home their promises and the points they are trying to make. Learn a few arm and hand movements that seem natural to you. If you need to put your hands in your pockets, that's okay, too, because it helps you look comfortable onstage. *But don't start and end that way.* Use it as one form of gesture mixed with others. Beware. If your hands stay in your pockets at all times, it's just as bad as standing still the whole time.

There's more! As I said, I could (and will) write a whole book just on this subject of monotony. For now, I leave you with these SRDs you can use immediately.

Presenter SRDs

- Start and end with distinct eye contact. Memorize your opening and closing, directing the words straight at your audience members without looking down at your notes.

- Start with a personal story. Allow attendees to get to know your personality. Give them a chance to connect and relate to you as a person before launching into your detailed content.

115

- Enunciate and practice changing your vocal patterns. Vary your pitch and tempo, and your content will come across as more interesting.

- Know your material. The more comfortable you are with the content, the more you can focus on the audience. It doesn't have to be memorized word for word, but know where it's going. Be ready to speak off the cuff when needed. That way, it looks and feels as if you're on the improvisation stage and talking freely—as experts do.

- Uncomfortable with taking a pause? Place a drink of water nearby and use the time it takes to grab a quick sip to pause a moment.

- The worst gestures are those that look rehearsed. For example, you emphatically claim, "And I believe this to be the best solution for our team right now!" Then you look down at your notes and realize . . . uh-oh . . . you forgot something. You look back at your audience, then strongly point your index finger to the ceiling in triumph. What just happened? You look foolish doing this gesture *after* delivering your big point. This may cause attendees to point at the ceiling or at you, except they might not use their pointer finger.

- When using humor or comedy, self-effacing humor is okay; making fun of others and embarrassing them is not. Don't do it.

- Look for ways to add humor every seven minutes, which is a natural learning cycle of the brain. Even a three-second mental break allows attendees to disengage enough for their brains to take a break, then reconnect.

- If you want to hold something in your hands when you present, ask for a hand microphone (wireless)

116

or a remote mouse. That will force you to stop fidgeting with other things. If you look nervous, you lose credibility.

• . Do you want attendees to write something down? Then build in dramatic pauses . . . [*pause*].

• Stay away from long technical words as much as you possibly can.

• If you look up after reading for five full minutes and no one is looking at you, something needs to change.

For a truly excellent resource to help you become a better presenter, join a Toastmasters chapter in your area. This group has helped millions of people become better presenters—and each and every one of their coworkers are eternally grateful. Visit www.Toastmasters.org to find a Toastmasters chapter near you.

Unreadable Slides Suck

The next time I feel like reading a book, why don't I just come to your meeting?

This is not a "have-you-ever-had-that-feeling?" moment; it's a "how-many-times-this-week-have-you-had-that-feeling?" question.

What's even worse than reading your PowerPoint slides? Having far too many words on a slide or having text that can't be discerned by attendees.

It's proven knowledge that meeting attendees have had enough of this malpractice. Unfortunately and regretfully, there's no insurance against it, yet this abuse occurs on a massive scale daily. Even executives with supposedly "the best of the best" experience can't seem to get the basics right.

I once gave a keynote presentation at a meeting for one of the major consulting firms in the world. Speaking immediately ahead of me was an executive vice president of HR presenting a new learning and resource system. She based her presentation on a long parade of slides (PowerPoint).

I'll give her credit for having an engaging personality, but energy and engagement were lost each time a slide changed. Why? Because she turned her back to read the slide she was about to present. And each slide averaged 200 words!

How many words is that? Well, from the heading "Unreadable Slides Suck" to the number 200 in the last paragraph is about 200 words. Now, conveying all this information on one slide and having people follow it is mission impossible.

This also goes for too many graphics or charts that have an absurd amount of detail. Oh, and colors. Ever try reading text that is yellow on a light-colored background? How about a shadowed blue on black? Color can be a powerful tool. Colors can evoke emotions (e.g., red is associated with anger and green with calm). Choosing the right ones can set up different moods and affect your audience in different, intentional ways. But having a colorful slide doesn't trump sheer visibility of the content. You don't have to be a professional graphic designer to figure it out. Just keep to the fundamentals—especially readability—and your presentation won't suck.

Presenter SRDs

- Make only one point on each slide. This is not a document; it's the background to a presentation that you're making. If you want to write a book, use another program.

- If you have to use text, use no more than *five words per line* and no more than *five lines per slide*. Remember, make yourself whittle down your message into key words. When I'm using PowerPoint, I don't put more than five words on any one slide unless I'm using a direct quote.

- Keep the letters large so everyone can see the wording in the back of the room. Stay at a 30-point size for most common fonts and increase point size from there, with titles typically being larger than text.

- Highlight or circle key data in a detailed graph or chart. If you must use a chart or graph with a lot of detail, use the highlighter, marker, or other tools to graphically circle the key facts or figures the audience should focus on. Don't talk about the data; attendees will be searching on the slide for the figures you're talking about instead of focusing their attention on why those numbers are important. (You are explaining why they're important, right?)

- Split large charts and graphs into small segments if necessary. Otherwise, audience members will have *no hope* of deciphering what they mean to them.

- Review the PowerPoint templates included with the software. They provide acceptable predefined color schemes for you to use so you don't have to make up your own.

- When using graphics in your presentation, choose colors from the graphics as your text colors to give the slide a consistent and professional look.

- Use color combinations that create a high contrast for ease of reading. PowerPoint defaults suggest white on black, violet on yellow, light green on purple, and blue/green on red.

- Test your colors on the projector you will be using to verify they will work on that projector.

- Don't use decorative, flashy, or extreme fonts except in a large header or for a two-word attention-getting line. Overuse the fonts and they'll lose their impact.

- Your main content text should be easy to read and clear at any size. Serif fonts generally appear more formal and can sometimes be difficult to read on large screens, whereas sans serif fonts are easy to read onscreen and appear more informal.

> **Times New Roman and Palatino are serif fonts; Calibri and Arial are sans serif.**

Remember, people have come to listen to *you*, the presenter. They haven't taken time out of their busy day to try to read unreadable text on a giant screen. If you simply start reading from your slides, so will everyone else—and you've just started your very own book club. If your ego needs that to fit your role in the organization, congratulations, you are there. But good luck getting your attendees to add comments, show up on time, or go out of their way to get there. Why should they when they can simply read about it in the morning paper.

Cutesy Moving Graphics Suck

Okay, it's time to fess up. If you've spent more time on making sure the graphical arrow spins and changes color to show a change in revenue than on your presentation skills, your meeting sucks!

Don't rely on artificial intelligence (like moving Power-Point graphics) to give the meeting emphasis when your boss is paying *you* to do it. Do your job!

The cutesy clip art images that jump and dance were cool back in the early 1990s when the new technology dazzled everyone and saved us from transparencies. Perhaps you were drawn to the screen to see how creative you could be with these cutesy graphics. Now, don't confuse this with adding pictures, video, flash, or music to help make your point. This can enhance your presentation.

Frankly, it perturbs me to know that someone took all that extra time to illustrate an emphatic point on a slide when it could and should have been done by the presenter in person! Ever heard of enunciating, showing enthusiasm, and building anticipation while giving a presentation? That's your job. Don't count on the cutesy revolving dollar signs to signify where the company needs to be next quarter.

Another thing that perturbs me is continually using moving backgrounds in your PowerPoint show. You'll find these on high-end custom presentations, and you can easily purchase templates that use them. While they may work on a title slide, if you keep that motion going through the whole presentation, then you better bring some motion-sickness pills—attendees will need them.

Wait, I think those pills cause drowsiness. Well, most meetings do, too, so what do you have to lose?

Presenter SRDs

- Use images and media to arouse emotion. Back that up by spending more time on your content, and stop relying on moving graphics to illustrate your point.

- Take a minute to determine how your attendees can get involved in any given slide. Possibly pose a question that directly relates to it and completes the picture mentally or physically.

- Try one approach at a time. If you're filling your screen with multiple graphics or photos on top of photos, it's time to redesign.

- If you're using animation, then keep it simple. Let the text fade in or fade out in the same spot it should appear. No need to display a double-twisted backflip to show your next step in the production cycle.

- Don't use a different animation effect on each slide transition (unless you are in third grade and your fellow students judge you on that).

- *Stop* using basic clip art. If I see you using the clip art of the guy looking through the magnifying glass from 1994, then you'll be fired and removed from this planet.

Trust me, if you are doing a professional or business presentation and you think the 3D text and revolving words that sparkle, zip in, or box out are cool, then your PowerPoint presentation sucks! And your audience will think you're an idiot.

Agenda Item 6

Make the Best of Sucky Meetings . . . or Get Out While You Can

Meetings take place in various form and fashions. From your project team check-ins to idea-generating sessions, meetings take place on the phone, Internet, video, and even in person. Each has its specific place in our working world, but no matter the type, the format, or the intended purpose, each can be abused.

Whatever meeting type you find yourself in, Agenda Item 6 helps you and your team launch the Bore No More! movement and learn to *get more*, so you can *get it done and get out*!

Never-Ending Meetings Suck

You're looking at your watch again, wishing the speaker would look at *his* watch. Doesn't he realize it's 4:45 on Friday afternoon, well beyond the posted 4:30 end time? You still have an important e-mail to compose, edit, and send before you can go home for the weekend.

You look around and read the same thing on everyone's faces: *We've accomplished all we possibly can in this meeting.* Like you, the other eight people around your conference table are conspiring to end this meeting so everyone can finish up and get out for the weekend.

Yet here you sit, tuning out Long-Winded Louie and wishing desperately to be back at your desk. Now it's 5 PM, and he's still going with no conclusion in sight.

Why do never-ending meetings happen? Oh, there are more reasons than are listed here, I know, but let's start with these:

- Poor chairperson facilitation

- Little or no preparation

- Too many items to talk about with not enough time planned

- Low activity from participants in the meeting, thus lack of progress on achieving the goals of the meeting or reaching any consensus

- Tangents (see "Dogs Who Get Off the Leash Suck" under Agenda Item 4)

- Distractions (see "Distractions Suck" under Agenda Item 7)

- Delays to make the meeting look like participants are accomplishing something so they don't actually have to do anything

Who's to blame for those horrid never-ending meetings? You! Yup, you're to blame because you allow these reasons to dictate what happens.

A driving theme of this book is that, as a meeting attendee, you and your colleagues have rights and responsibilities. Your collective job is not to sit there in silence like lame ducks. Your job is to take an active role in any meeting you attend. If you're not facilitating the meeting, you might believe you have *no right* to do anything about what goes on in that meeting. In fact, you have every right.

While every meeting (we hope) has a stated purpose with defined objectives, not every meeting stays on its intended course. Whether one attendee forces the conversation down an unplanned path (with lots of personal baggage tagging along) or the group realizes something new is needed to accomplish the task at hand, the facilitator has to address unexpected challenges. Either way, it's a predicament of time. *Your* time. And it's in danger of being wasted.

Rarely do you see invites to meetings that list *only* a start time. Correct me if I'm wrong, but most meetings typically have a time frame clearly stated, such as "2:00 to 3:00 PM," right? Therefore you can assume that the meeting was *intended* to end at some point. But in never-ending meetings, the facilitator might be dealing with any of the following:

- A poor perception of how long it would take to accomplish the desired objectives

- A lack of ability or experience to manage the agenda

- Disruptive attendees who come unprepared, who are naysayers, or who initiate "dogs off the leash" behavior (see Agenda Item 4).

- Poor interpersonal skills to confront that inevitable person who hijacks the meeting by forcing it into a new, time-wasting direction

Never-ending meetings are endemic—so much so that I coined a term for them: the *cream cheese factor*. It's

125

simply this: Inevitably, the longer the meeting persists, the longer the cream cheese sits out and gathers bacteria, and thus the more inedible it becomes.

Just as your quality-decision-making ability and creative juices diminish the longer you are trapped within the four-walled closet of the conference room, the cream cheese factor can prevail when your meeting isn't engaging or well facilitated.

Here is the basic *cream cheese factor* rundown:

5- to 15-minute meeting: You experience a cool, crisp cream cheese taste along with a nice clean knife to cut and spread it.

15- to 45-minute meeting: You're settled in. Cheese is entirely spreadable, but the choices on best flavors might be running low.

45- to 90-minute meeting: Cheese may have a good schmear factor, but you have to scrape the remnants of the strawberry and blueberry flavors.

90-minute to 3-hour meeting: It's a bit dried and crusty, but edible. You might want to think about throwing away what's left.

3- to 5-hour meeting: Eat at your own risk.

All-day meeting: Eat what's left of the unpopular onion flavor, and you'll regret it tomorrow.

Looking at your watch again? Realizing that no one else is going to finish the budget updates that you are on the hook for? Ready to get out gracefully? Use the following SRDs.

Attendee SRDs

Here are polite ways to push facilitators and fellow attendees who have settled in to letting the cream cheese get moldy. Your goal is to wrap up the meeting and either Get It Done or Get Out.

Know this: The moment you employ these SRDs around colleagues who are part of the Bore No More! movement, they will join you and help ensure the meeting ends on time.

- Before the meeting starts, read through the agenda and ask yourself, "Do I understand my role and why I'm here to support this agenda and this group?" If this hasn't been stated in the agenda or other pre-meeting communication, then it's fair to ask the facilitator this question (preferably via text or e-mail well before the meeting begins): "How can I best help in this meeting today, Frank? What's my role?" Frank might reply that he or "the powers that be" want you to hear the information. At this point, you're likely suffering from the overinvitation syndrome. Apply the SRDs throughout this book and ask Frank (or whoever wants you there) to send you the relevant information *after* the meeting.

- Most of the time, never-ending meetings just happen. Therefore, if you find yourself faced with 10 minutes remaining on the clock for the planned departure time, yet several agenda items haven't been touched, spring into action. If the facilitator won't address the dwindling time or acknowledge an appalling lack of progress—or both—then *you* need to take on that responsibility. Do so in a helpful tone of voice. Avoid attacking or making your statement in an aggressive manner. That will backfire on you. Politely say to the facilitator, "Frank, this has been great. We have only 10 minutes until we have to leave, and I want to make sure we get to resolutions for X, Y, and Z.

127

When do we want to schedule time to review A, B, and C and finalize X, Y, and Z?"

- Five minutes to go and no end in sight? Try this: Look around the table and say, "Frank, before everyone packs up and loses track of what we accomplished, let's recap the key action items here. Let's restate what we got through and determine a plan to discuss items still on the table." With luck, Frank will get the point and begin the official meeting wrap-up. If not, then act in a proactive (and nonthreatening) way and recap it from your notes or from the owner of the "pass the pad" responsibilities (see "Starting Late Sucks" in Agenda Item 4). Get through the wrap-up, review action items, and assign responsibility for them. Also note any parking lot issues.

- When all this succeeds—or even when it fails—and no wrap-up is looming, then with one minute remaining, *stand up*. That's right. Quietly, simply, stand up. Don't pack up or start unplugging your laptop. Just stand up and maintain eye contact with people in the room. It's a powerful signal that you're about to leave, yet still willing to handle anything that needs to be addressed. Do you understand how awesome it can be when six of your nine meeting members stand up at 2:59 PM and everyone "gets" why you're doing this? This tactic is extremely effective when done appropriately and not rudely. Think of the Oscars or Emmy ceremonies when music interrupts what a long-winded award winner is saying. Like the music, standing up is the signal. (Yup, certain ground rules must apply. If your CEO is about to reveal the fiscal results for last year, think twice about standing up at the one-minute mark.)

128

- If you're in the middle of a meeting and a new item comes up that legitimately needs to be addressed but is not relevant to your role there, then respectfully ask, "What time would you like us back to continue our agenda?" (Avoid saying cynically, "*Do* you want us to come back?") Or offer the option for someone to text you when attendees are ready for you to present the reports you've prepared. Do this whether or not the meeting is turning into a never-ending extravaganza of non-information. Protect your time.

Facilitator SRDs

When you must facilitate a meeting, apply the following SRDs.

- Be realistic in your expectations. Can you really conquer eight major items in 60 minutes with 11 people in the room adding commentary and confusion? Always opt to go with four items and *end early* rather than race to deal with eight items and finish only four. The feeling of closure and accomplishment far outweighs that extra 20 minutes of babble you planned to present.

- Schedule it before lunch. Everyone wants out in time for lunch.

- If you see you'll have to finish past your meeting's end time, bring it to the attention of the group. Don't leave them in limbo. *You can't keep going as if nothing happened and no one noticed.* Trust me, everyone in the room knows you're over the time limit long before you realize it. That's why you need the group's buy-in to continue or to make other arrangements. Set parameters and respect your attendees' time; presume they are committed to be elsewhere

129

and they're staying only by choice. A few tips to consider:

- Give them the opportunity to reschedule other items so they can remain in your meeting.

- Specify which items you will be completing and how and when you will address the other items.

- Tackle the issues that will take the longest or require everyone's buy-in first. Think about what items you can still address if Craig from the facilities team or Jo from accounting needs to leave. Save small items that you and Mary can work out after the meeting or over coffee the next morning.

- Be the authority in the room and stick to your guns (or cream-cheese-laden knife) to get things done. Don't let your meeting be usurped by Tangent Tom or Fred the Funny Man.

- If a true meeting stopper comes up that needs to be addressed before you can continue, then discuss it but specify how the agenda will change. If you can let half of the attendees return to their offices, then *do it*! Ask them to come back by a certain time, or say you'll text them when they're needed.

- Prepare to save the last 10 minutes for final resolution, wrap-up, and confirmation of who will cover which action items. Don't let this be an afterthought when you have only two minutes left, or worse, when you've already exceeded your time limit.

Do you like to hear the sound of your own voice and thus become the cause of too many never-ending meetings? If that's you, stop jumping on other people's words and start listening. When you have that urge to interrupt

(I know, it's an overwhelming urge to point out that someone is wrong . . . or to finish the speaker's sentence . . . or to better articulate the sentence . . . or to express your extremely valuable opinion), well, take a breath and then write down your thought so it doesn't get lost. Really, maybe the person will address it in the next few minutes. If that doesn't happen, wait to speak in turn. I'm not kidding about this. (If you need homework to reinforce this, read Dale Carnegie's best-seller *How to Win Friends and Influence People*.)

- Ask questions instead of making direct comments. That way, you'll gain a better understanding in place of spouting off every ancillary comment you think all should be aware of.

- Trust that if people have questions, they'll ask them. The point is this: You want to understand exactly how you can contribute to the effectiveness of any meeting.

- To save yourself the headache of getting caught in a meeting in which you don't belong, arrange a departure point with the facilitator or meeting host. Politely proclaim that you've performed your obligation to the best of your ability, thank the meeting host, and then leave. No reason to take on roles you're not needed for at the risk of stalling the process. Do your part and move on.

Out of politeness, people stay in meetings to hear about other facets of an issue that don't affect them. Then they complain about the time spent in that meeting, forgetting who had decided to stay!

If you have a clear understanding of your role and a comfort level to withdraw when your game is over, then do so. Don't feel ashamed; be proud. People respect you for your valiant participation in the meeting and for keeping them focused on the next salient item.

> **Oh, and one more thing. If you do have an all-day meeting, please, *please*, refresh the cream cheese often.**

Déjà Meetings Suck

Ever had the feeling you've been in this meeting before? Oh my gosh, you have, and too many times.

You're in a meeting—same people, same room, even the same dang report as last week. You've been driven to create a spreadsheet that has Las Vegas–style odds, whereby members can gamble real dollars if Steady Steve reports anything new (*always* bet against it), or if Repeat Rhonda asks the same questions as last time, or if Missed-It Michael asks outright, "What happened in the last meeting I missed?"

As an attendee, why do you stand for the déjà meeting syndrome? Complacency, perhaps? Feel you don't have the ability to do anything about it? Because your boss is holding the meeting and you're better off to grin and bear it?

If you've actively presented in past meetings and always come prepared, *you have rights*! Those rights allow you to speak up for this continued massive abuse of time—yours and your coworkers'—especially with all the real work you have on your plate.

If there ever was a time for mutiny, this is it. That's right. *Power to the people*! Someone must say *something* about boring déjà meetings. Hey, after all, it's the Bore No More! movement, right?

As a facilitator or chairperson or attendee, how can you possibly allow yet another déjà meeting? Does it require standing up to your arch nemesis, or possibly creating some hardship? Does it take too much time preparing something new for the next meeting?

If you want to show lack of respect for your fellow attendees' time, then play into this trap: Your boss, Micromanaging Melissa, shows up and pulls her stereotypical "too important and busy to show up last time," and she is now on a fact-finding mission to hijack your meeting and asks you to give her a rundown of what she missed. Know this: She didn't take the time to read the meeting notes from last time.

Rehashing or explaining things that have taken place in a past meeting is a top complaint among meeting participants. Déjà meetings generally happen because someone wasn't at the last meeting and wants to know what he or she missed. Or too much time has passed since the last meeting and no good notes exist. It's okay, maybe, to recap the action items from the last meeting, but taking the time to explain, discuss, debate, and rehash the same boring details handled the first time around is *not*.

To be fair, it could be that since the last meeting, the environment or data has changed and decisions made previously would now carry a high risk. Or it could be that an attendee wants one more shot at influencing the group. Much of this comes under the human factor, which then risks political or emotional repercussions if handled poorly. (This element is addressed in the SRDs.)

133

What can you do? Do you risk getting fired by telling your boss to be quiet? Do you kick out Melissa and the brownnoses who jump on her "let's-talk-about-last-time" bandwagon? Do you politely refer them to the Web page that has all the details? Let's look at the following points and see how we can reduce the suckification with this ongoing problem.

Attendee SRDs

Self-moderators of the world, unite! If your meeting chairperson allows the meeting to flow into déjà meeting mode, take these suggestions:

- If it's a large meeting, then leave. If any colleagues are sticking around, have them text you when it's time to return. Seriously. (Disclaimer: Some restrictions apply, as always.)

- If you have the clout and confidence, don't take control, but shift the control in the right direction by asking the meeting facilitator, "Do you have the minutes from last time that we can give to No-Show Nolan so we can all be on the same page?" It's a gentle reminder to the guy who's threatening to push the meeting into the place no one wants to go that you're not buying it. Offer to share last meeting's minutes and let him catch up on his own.

- Leave your items on the table and ask the facilitator to "text me when we're back on next year's budget instead of last month's (or whatever item applies to you), as I have a quick call to return." Chances are that the facilitator will get the point and get back on track.

- Get a room! Tell déjà team members, "Steve and I are going to the conference room next door to start on action item two while you review last week's items."

- Feeling even more gutsy? Boss in the room? Then simply slide down to the other end of the table and mention to those not involved in the déjà meeting, "Let's get these other items knocked out." Leave it at that. Send the message that you are going to remain productive; if they want to join you, then they're welcome to come along.

Facilitator SRDs

- Make the previous meeting's notes and action items readily accessible. As the meeting chairperson or facilitator, assuming you followed up after the last meeting and proper action items and notes are available and posted, be certain to document where they are, or include them with the next meeting invitation. Whether they are available via the *notes only* part of the agenda, a dedicated folder on the server, or the group Web or wiki page, you must make the details accessible to everyone.

- If someone asks you what happened in the last meeting, and you have failed to provide the info, then you are at fault.

- Empower your people to come prepared. If they had access to the information and didn't follow through, then you own the power. Upon their request to rehash the discussion or outcomes from last meeting, you can:

  - Pass them the documentation (provided you were feeling generous before the meeting, expected this, and printed it out).

  - Quickly forward the e-mail or link from your phone, and keep the meeting going without missing a beat.

135

- Share with them that the information is in the meeting notes, and if they want to go grab them quickly, that's fine.

> **Déjà meetings seem as common as the common cold—we're all subjected to them, but we have no real cure for them.**

I'm not a fan of embarrassing anyone in front of others by making that person look like an unprepared fool. I personally think that is uncalled for, and it will foster animosity against you as coworker or add to a feeling of resentment. In the end, embarrassing someone will only hurt the effectiveness of your meetings.

I am a fan of those attendees knowing that they are expected to come prepared. You want your attendees to know that you do your premeeting planning with certain expectations in mind, and if they choose not to do their homework, then they'll have to catch up on their own. It's not a reason to hold the rest back.

If you decide to draw a line in the sand on all abuses of your time, and if you wish to put a few items on your abuse-prevention list, déjà meetings are solid candidates for that list. It takes guts for an attendee to get a meeting back on track, but remember that meetings aren't ends unto themselves. You're there to accomplish something, so go for it.

Project and Update Meetings Suck

If you've ever worked on a detailed project, or even a simple project, with an overbearing leader, you know what

I'm talking about. A major time waster is the regularly scheduled project or update meeting. What's the primary purpose of this type of meeting? Having a collective group of people share information so that each participant knows the overall status or milestones affecting their work. Is it important? Heck, yeah! If you have a milestone that depends on others completing their tasks, and their task orientation has changed in scope or deadline, you need to know about it. It colors everything from your daily work plan to the outcome of the project.

Unfortunately, many of these status meetings simply rehash or confirm what you already know. You know you're in the land of project-meeting abuse if you find yourself thinking, "My report to the group will be the same as last time. Please, not another déjà meeting. I'm on schedule. My team is doing what we said we'd do. Do I really need to be there?"

You may have one of those project managers who feels he or she needs to have a meeting, no matter what, so that it looks like he or she is keeping up. Yup, been there!

Jim Canterucci is an expert in project management and author of *Change Project Management: The Next Step* and the Amazon.com best-seller *Personal Brilliance*. Jim points out that the attributes that make project managers successful tend to carry over to the meeting environment. Meeting leadership skills can sell ideas, build coalitions, obtain additional resources, facilitate decision making, obtain objective status reports, communicate project status, and resolve project issues. Your degree of success in all of these areas is significantly affected by how effective—or how boring—the meetings you conduct are!

Jim, thanks for building the case for this book.

137

Folks, one of the most common problems for project managers is the de facto regularly scheduled and infamous "project meeting." Alarm bells should go off if even the mere thought crosses your mind, "I wonder if we need this meeting today?" Not only do you struggle for a reason to have it, but you probably struggle to find any resulting action at its conclusion. If you're the project leader, cancel a few regularly scheduled meetings and see whether anyone notices or complains. If that's not an option, then try the following alternatives.

Facilitator SRDs

- The best-revered advice for regular status or project meetings at the same time on the same channel is this: Please, oh please, change the channel. To do that, make a team decision to change your format to a "Two 'n Out" or "Step It Up" meeting style (see Agenda Item 3).

- If you can't use alternative-style meetings all the time, have your "Two 'n Out" two or three weeks of the month; the third and/or fourth week, return to your regularly scheduled program to address the bigger picture.

- Lose your ego and craving for that extra special weekly love. Just let your people do their jobs. You know the ones who need handholding, anyway. Don't feel the need to call a meeting just to *have* a meeting so others believe you're doing *your* job.

- Canceling a meeting, however, can't be used as an excuse for communication breakdowns or missed milestones. Keep track of your tasks and the milestones reached for each subproject. Keep members informed, using their preferred means to cover

138

progress and milestone accomplishments. Do this, and your people will stay informed and appreciate gaining back an hour otherwise wasted in an unnecessary meeting.

- All team members are certainly capable of providing status updates via SharePoint services, a company intranet page, or a shared folder. Or, use a software based program such as Microsoft Project or Basecamp as mentioned in Agenda Item 2. Need to track the progress of a milestone that affects your status? Go check it. No need to circle the wagons.

- If the project cycle is long, request a written update from each team leader specifically targeting details related to any deviation from the original project plan. These updates allow you to plan or revise your meeting schedules and strategize which people need to attend these meetings.

Attendee SRDs

If you're a regular attendee of your team's update meetings, pay attention to the following tips.

- Explain that you are on target with all milestones and no changes since the last meeting. If all you have are noncritical updates such as "everything is going as planned," simply provide your meeting host with that information. If you do have questions or critical items to report and need questions answered, then suit up, 'cuz it's meetin' time.

- If the regular meetings are blurring content and depleting energy, suggest alternative meeting types, or implement the "Pass the Buck" style meeting discussed in Agenda Item 3. That allows you to lead the

139

next meeting with renewed energy and focus. From wherever you sit around the table, don't let your meeting suck.

> ### Get Out!
>
> - If you have multiple subteams within a project team, then suggest meeting with only your respective team members if the boss requires regular meetings. No need to get updates on items that don't apply to you.
>
> - When all team members must meet, send only one representative from your respective group. No need to send five when one person can address the questions and update the subteam. Assign a different person each time for this task. This approach saves time for others in the group and improves group productivity.

Project and update meetings should focus your team on what needs to be done and keep everyone motivated toward the common goal. Make it about future plans, not past problems. Save those past problem comments for posting in the project team folder—or on the stall door in the bathroom.

Scattered Showers' Meetings Suck

The scene is set. You might have been called to do one of the following:

- Generate thoughts on what the company's new web site should be.

- Determine the best ways to build team morale and unity.

- Develop new ideas for the marketing campaign.

Yes, you're off and running in the classic brainstorming meeting.

> **Yet if the whiteboard ends up white, you have nothing more than partly cloudy skies.**

What's the goal of a brainstorming meeting? Its main impetus is the belief that lots of people can generate more ideas in a short amount of time by using ideas that come up to trigger even more ideas. This format also helps participants bond around a common goal and increases their commitment to the outcome. Besides, it's social and can be upbeat and fun—especially for those who don't get out much.

Group sourcing for ideas can be rewarding in big and small ways. At the same time, it's critical to keep inherent problems in mind to avoid your brainstorming meeting from sucking all the moisture from the space around you.

What can make a brainstorming meeting ineffective? Let's start with:

- Poor facilitation

- Pathetic follow-up on the ideas

- Poor time management of meeting (lasts too long)

- Low level of participation from attendees

- Lack of focus because discussion isn't narrow enough

- Too many people talking over one another so no one can hear

141

- Emphasis on evaluating ideas that come up instead of generating new ones

The biggest problem with brainstorming meetings centers on what happens to the ideas generated, which is often *nothing*. Lack of follow-up could be due to laziness or inexperience. Many times, it can be because your leader had an idea in mind to begin with, but wanted to pretend that "the group came up with it." Then, you expand on your (excuse me, the leader's) idea and everyone feels involved in the process. (If *you* are this manager, stop wearing your *me-me-me* mantra on your sleeve. Instead, open fully to a group decision!)

Also, if you want to generate a mass of ideas from a variety of sources or demographics, it's wise to access greater spheres of influence. With the easy ability to poll for feedback and post comments, why limit yourself to the mere mortals gathered around you? Assuming you can talk publicly about the subject, open it up to the world. If not, at least open it up internally to those in your entire organization (if appropriate). Intranet, wikis, and internal project pages work well, as long as people know what's available and participation is encouraged. In this environment, you don't even need to set the meeting time. Go ahead and "Triple T" your meeting now (see Agenda Item 3).

Facilitator SRDs

If you're destined to lead the classic brainstorming meeting, follow these solid SRDs to a "T."

- Keep the scope specific. The more detail you can include about the meeting's desired outcome or concept, the more detailed and on target the responses. Wide-open topics of discussion will get wide-open results with less chance of real traction. If you have multiple topics to address, break them into separate sessions, or discuss them on different days or in different online folders.

- Keep the idea generation focused and short. There's no time for tangents. Most people don't often engage in creative thinking; they tend to do their jobs the way they've always done them. Besides, using the other half of the brain takes energy. In the meeting, when ideas dry up, move on or ask clarifying questions. Idea selection and evaluation happens after the idea generation and will require additional time.

- State ground rules and suggested timing up front. Aim to spend 10 minutes on generating multiple ideas, 10 minutes expanding and enhancing viable ones, 10 minutes selecting the finalists, and then 30 minutes evaluating top selections.

- New ideas come at any time, not just when you're in a brainstorming meeting. Encourage texting or messaging ideas you can add to the selection list later. Why can't the morning shower be the brainstorm location of choice?

- No fire-hosing! That's when a participant shares an idea and someone jumps all over it with a "been-there-done-that-didn't-work" comment. Remember, you never want to put out the fire of *any* ideas. There is an idea-generation phase and an evaluation phase, so stay true to both. If you want people to clam up and stop sharing ideas, allow someone to hose initial ideas. This results in two things: hurt feelings and a wealth of squashed ideas.

- When face-to-face brainstorming groups are more than 10 people, break into smaller groups. Why? Because it's easy for people and ideas to hide in large groups. It also evokes fear of being ridiculed in front of an audience.

143

Generate ideas *within small groups* and collect the best ones for the selection and evaluation phase.

- Want increased participation? Ask group members to bring with them at least three starter ideas. This helps beat the "Tom-already-said-my-idea" excuse heard in idea-generation sessions.

- When everyone is blurting out that first batch of ideas that come so freely, it can be tough for one person to write them all down. Have two or more scribes take notes, and ask people to direct their comments to one person or the other. Another option: Pull out your smart phone and hit the "memo record" function. Scribes can listen to the playback and jot down ideas they missed.

- Find a creative space for brainstorming. Use other meeting styles, or try speed meetings, both of which are discussed in Agenda Item 3, to keep the blood flowing to the brain and to keep people active.

Attendee SRDs

- If the facilitator has not set up a focused element for brainstorming, ask clarifying questions to get to a finer point, and don't allow anyone to lose sight of it. Rewrite that focus at the top of the board, paper, or Web page header.

- If a plan wasn't shared about the process you'll be following, ask for one, and set a specific amount of time to be spent on each issue.

- If the facilitator doesn't stop the fire-hosing, jump in early and quickly with a question to the facilitator like this: "Are we finished with new ideas?" Do this every single time it's needed, even though people can finish the sentence for you.

144

- Bring a squirt gun and, whenever someone fire-hoses, ready . . . aim . . . *fire!* Having multiple guns in the room equals exponential fun. Just watch out. You don't want to ruin anyone's phone, or you'll have one extremely upset attendee!

Get Out!

If the meeting stalls and you want it to end, speak up, stand up, and ask the host, *"When* we get more ideas, what's the best way to share them with you?" Then make your polite departure to go *think* about those ideas.

If you want new ideas to be innovative, why not be innovative in the way you develop them? Get in the game of making a more productive and creative session by providing a format that fosters what you want. You can let the skies open up and flood the team with new ideas instead of simply clouding over with the same foggy results.

Conference Calls Suck

That's right, it's our favorite pastime! Conference calls are *the* excuse for a quick makeshift meeting with people in various locations. They're another example of perfectly good technology being used in all the wrong ways.

My main gripe with conference calls? They generally start with less planning than you use to select your morning breakfast cereal. And how does that leave you? As soggy and dull as your Cheerios after soakin' in milk for 90 minutes. Hmm, last time I checked, that would be about the

145

same length as your last conference call. And those are 90 minutes of your life you'll never get back.

I decided to take my own advice and find out what others thought about conference calls. I put the question out on to my social media network: "What's your biggest frustration when joining a conference call?" I received responses within a couple of minutes of posting. (I guess I touched on what many consider a stress point.) Do you agree with these aggravations?

- Moderators who don't know the meaning of *moderate* in their comments

- Keyboard pecking (listeners audibly typing away on their computers)

- Not knowing who's speaking because the moderator or speaker doesn't make it clear

- When people think they've hit mute and start chatting away (thus inadvertently revealing a lot of personal stuff)

- Having to put up with the stinkin' beeping sound, no matter what you do

- When no one on the call is engaged—*no one*!

- When you reschedule to accommodate someone and that person *still* doesn't show up on the call

- The classic sign-off line, "Call me, after we hang up" (duh . . . thus implying that he or she has something to say and doesn't want others to hear)

- When the host asks, "Who's on?" and everyone tries to figure out when it's his or her turn to say something

- Asking someone a question and getting dead silence because that person either left or is on mute

- Seeing Facebook posts and tweets from people on the call (ironically, because the person who posted this did so while on a conference call)

- Conference call attendees who have the speaker-phone so *loud* that others can hear it in their cubicles or offices

One person wrote, "I always ask if anyone has any questions before we go. And, of course, I get silence. But as soon as we hang up, here come all the e-mails with questions. Aarrggh!" (I feel your frustration, Chrissy.)

Another caller stated this as one of her worst frustrations: "Why don't people realize that if they are listening to the call and need to put *our* call on hold, *everyone else* hears the 'on-hold' music? It's awful!" Just to make her point (and mine), let's join a conference call already in progress.

As we continue to talk about the value that our customer will be seeing, I would like to . . . [*enter Muzak background music . . . I'm leaving on a jet plane*] um . . . share that when Steve and I [. . . *don't know when I'll . . .*] were . . . um . . . presenting to our first focus group last week [. . . *be back again . . .*] Uh [. . . *baby, I hate to go . . .*]

Can everyone still hear me?

Okay. Now try this one on for size:

. . . I have the portal section of the site almost [*tappity*] done, but our [*tap-tap*] initial scope [*tip-tap*] of services [*tap-tap-tappity-tap*] didn't actually cover [*woof- woof!*]

147

the new ideas that the client wants to now do. We are [*obnoxious ring tone . . . screams!*] talking about some major scope [*ba-bleep*] creep here . . . uh, who just joined?

It's Tim.

Thanks, Tim. What I was saying was that we'll have some major scope creep if we don't . . .

Hey, can I call you back?

. . . go back to the client [*bzzzzzz-bzzzzzz*] and take care of this. [*Now boarding . . . Flight 1-2-3 . . .*]

Don't you agree, Stacey? Stacey?

Yeah. Well, I believe so, but I was uh . . . mute-challenged [*tip-tap*] there for a minute. Can you rephrase that? I want to make sure I heard you correctly.

I *said*, how are we going to . . . [*ba-bleep*]

Hi, sorry I'm late. It's Jon.

Uh . . . Jon, what are we going to do about it?

About what? What are we talking about?

Do I really need to continue here? You live this every day. You can see a hysterical scenario of something similar by searching "Dave Grady conference call" on YouTube, or simply click through to it from the www.BoringMeetings Suck.com web site. It's well worth listening to and shows exactly what I'm talking about!

Rudeness like this occurs on *most* conference calls that you host, set up, or attend as a participant—and don't even try to deny it! The background sounds of mobile gadgets play in harmony as texts, typing, doorbells, barking dogs, ring tones, on-hold music, and even the sound effects from the game on your iPad are abundant. Nearly as frequent as the basic conference-call malpractices are botched calls that happen because people don't know how to hold them or how to set them up and run them. Let's examine these points.

Why would you have conference calls? Well, with tight budgets, free conference services widely available, and ad hoc meetings being set up quickly, conference calls are considered the most efficient way to accomplish an objective while keeping people at their desks and squeezing the meeting into an already overburdened schedule. Here's the good news. Conference calls can be a great "Get In, Get It Done, and Get Out" style of meeting. With good basic facilitation skills and an understanding of how to use them in a virtual environment, these calls can be highly beneficial.

Facilitator SRDs

How can you set up conference calls effectively? Is it even possible? Here are a few SRDs (there are many more) to consider when you're facilitating a conference call.

- See "Starting Late Sucks" in Agenda Item 4. Apply, rinse, and repeat.

- Do I really need to mention the detailed agenda that was sent at least 24 hours ahead of time? Really, do I?

- Identify and state your clear goal up front, and stay on track diligently. If you want most of your callers to tune out quickly, get on a tangent that doesn't involve them. Good luck getting them back; they're deep into something else by now.

- More than ever, vary the tone and pace of your voice. If you're moderately boring in a real-life presentation, then you'll come across as *deadly boring* on the phone.

Make the Best of Sucky Meetings . . .

- Don't review information that's already been presented for the benefit of latecomers. If latecomers insist on knowing what's going on, immediately send notes directly to their e-mail, or text them the link where they can download your notes. Say, "Notes are on the way," and continue the meeting.

- As a host, use people's names as often as possible, even calling on them at times and directly eliciting a response:

  - "Great comment, Samantha. What do you think about that, Pat?"

  - "Tell us your thoughts on this, Tim."

  - "Tim, do you agree with Amy?"

  This tactic might surprise them—and either catch them off guard or trying to talk with the mute button on. Watch how the offender cleverly looks for a way to ask you to repeat the question. But no matter what, calling on Patricia will surely keep her more engaged going forward. It will also keep the others on edge, thinking you'll do the same to them (and you will). It's certainly better than being lost in the background.

- End the call clearly, and thank everyone for joining. If you are continuing with any discussions after the official conference call, know that eavesdropping listeners are possible, whether intentional (people curious) or unintentional (people waking up from the snooze you initiated). Often, people who realize they've overstayed their welcome are then even more embarrassed to hang up. They fear that the exit beep will alert everyone to their offense.

- Do what it takes to get the action items disseminated to all parties as quickly as possible following the call.

150

Out of sight, out of mind. Most conference systems allow recordable conferences and an easy MP3 download. Get it, send it, and file it to a public location where attendees can retrieve it.

Attendee SRDs

- Watercooler conversations, which seem necessary in personal meetings, don't work if everyone isn't involved. Get your gossip and your drink elsewhere.

- Not everyone recognizes your voice. Introduce yourself before speaking for the first few times or as necessary. This is especially helpful with a new group or team, and it's immensely helpful for the note taker of the group.

- If you're late, don't announce it and interrupt someone in midsentence. That person already heard the *ba-bleep* sound and knows someone is there. Just keep quiet. You know people are itching to be the first to yell out, "Who just joined?" This happens to be the most abused phrase on conference calls today, immediately followed by, "Sorry, but I have to jump off."

- Invest in a quality headset that softens background noise. If you must work on your keyboard in the background, at least don't let your conference call world know it.

- When in environments with a lot of background noise (cars, airports . . . when the wind is blowing through your golf cart), use your mute button.

- If you use the mute button to mask typing or the fact that you're on the golf course, *don't* forget about it when you attempt to speak. Dead silence after

151

someone asks you a question absolutely ensures you look like an idiot.

- *Do not* use the hold button unless you want all the others to be subjected to a poor rendition of "Leaving on a Jet Plane" or some such musical interlude.

- Turn off your call waiting option if you're taking the call from a phone with this capability. That *click-click* can interrupt the point someone is making.

- See how many spins you can make in your office chair with one push. Let's see if you can beat my record of 13—no extra pushes allowed.

Get Out!

- For those mass distribution calls you're required to listen to, pull down the recording after the call (as most are recorded) and play it in double time on your way home in traffic. There, I just saved you hours upon hours of your life right there!

- E-mail the call leader in advance, explaining you have another appointment at the same time, but you don't want to miss the call. Ask the leader to schedule your piece of information near the beginning of the call and address any questions. Then you've completed the task early, and you can bid your best farewell as you make it home on time for meatloaf and gravy.

- If your input will be needed later in the call, ask politely that someone text you when the time is right and offer to rejoin the call then. Odds are, you will never be contacted.

- Say *"I'm going . . . into a . . . t . . . tun . . . nel, I may lose . . ."* and hang up. This tactic fares well for the mountains, the countryside, and so on. It also works wonders if you sit next to a loud fan that can blow air into the receiver. The annoyance should soon be followed by a request for you to drop out because you're disturbing everyone else (*aah, perfect*).

With more people taking part in more conference calls worldwide, businesses can't afford for them to be unproductive. Suckification Reduction Devices (SRDs) will not only help you in the calls you host, but even in those that you didn't want to join in the first place. Here's one approach:

"Who just joined?"

"Jon did, so let's get this done!"

Sales Team Meetings Suck

Let me be clear about something: Sales managers who talk *at* their salespeople during sales meetings commit a compound infraction—time lost in the meeting plus time the salespeople could have been selling. But it gets worse. It takes at least the same amount of time to recover from a session of information overload as it took to hold the meeting in the first place. Yikes!

A sales meeting focuses your team members on common objectives, motivates them, and provides the necessary support for them to be more effective—that is, sell more. If you, as a sales manager, haven't fully planned your weakly (oops, I mean *weekly*) team meeting and instead ask for updates on what's in their pipeline, stop fooling yourself. That won't accomplish your purpose—not one bit. Here's what I've learned from my days as an inside sales rep in the software industry and as a vice president of sales in the insurance industry (with 52 offices): Most sales meetings suck! And if your team members are honest with their feedback, they'll tell you that, too.

I remember it well. *In a sales meeting far, far away . . . or maybe in the conference room next to your cube . . .*

Every Monday morning brought the inevitable weekly sales meeting at nine o'clock sharp! If you were late, the fearless and breathless sales manager (otherwise known as the Wind-Up Toy) would sic his assistant on you like Jo-Jo, the junkyard dog. You'd be called incessantly, until either you or your death certificate showed up.

Why call him "breathless"? The guy never inhaled! His whole meeting was a two-hour elongated exhale of babble driven by the tightly wound spring that had been twisted by his boss only moments before. It was as if someone wound him up, pushed him into the room, and slammed the door shut. The sales reps were captured, not captivated. With the exit at the front of the room, leaving required entering center stage to exit stage right. Imagine interrupting Wind-Up's performance. And that's exactly what our wind-up sales meetings were: a performance.

It's a waste of time to meet when the manager's standard comments come spewing forth at breakneck speed for no apparent reason. Comments include: *"The economy is . . ."; "This is what the market is doing . . ."; "This is what I heard . . .";* and *"You need to do more to reach our quota."* The big wind-up . . . and then the pitch!

Of course, salespeople aren't homogeneous drones who have exactly the same clients, goals, and issues. They aren't all at the same level of development, either. But the wind-up-toy sales manager thinks they are, so he vomits omniscient instructions all over everyone within earshot.

I found repeatedly that the promised "quick one-hour meeting" regularly turned into a two-hour deflating experience. No talking about real problems, no potty breaks, no ideas relevant to any particular situation—just a rant about our current offering of products sprinkled with famous quotes. Stale like a bag of chips lying open for three days.

After the performance, we'd shuffle back to our cubes and gradually creep back into reality, which struck after lunch. Our bright-and-early Mondays started around one in the afternoon.

In reality, a complete book can be written on the topic of sales meetings, so don't worry, I won't continue on this bumpy road. If you like in-your-face advice, with strong action items to back it up, you can't go wrong with Jeffrey Gitomer's work (www.Gitomer.com).

Facilitator SRDs

- If you don't have new, compelling content for your salespeople, then simply don't bog them down in meetings.

- In your remarks, focus on the sales *accomplishments*, not on the losses.

155

- Ask questions, because telling ain't selling. Sales managers who tell, tell, tell create salespeople who tell, tell, tell . . . and don't sell, sell, sell. Great salespeople engage buyers, build relationships, and listen, just like we should do at sales team meetings.

- Send a questionnaire to team members and find out where they need assistance and what struggles they're facing, then determine their needs or concerns. Base your meeting's agenda closely on their responses.

- Keep each meeting short—20 or 30 minutes at the most. They can't handle more. That's why they picked sales!

- If you want your salespeople to buy in to new strategies, help them come up with the ideas and formulate solutions, promotions, goals, or even incentive plans.

- If a salesperson needs remedial training, provide it one-on-one. Don't call a meeting of everyone to educate one. Hire the right people to begin with. The right people can read the product literature and training manuals and don't need a remedial course every week.

- Invite a guest from other departments once a month. Often, department heads believe the sales team is off playing golf and living on expense accounts. Help them understand what it takes to keep your shop running, including all the work and relationship building that go into even the smallest sales.

- Help your team understand what happens after the sale is made and what challenges emerge when proper procedures aren't followed.

156

- Scheduling a meeting just because it's Monday morning? Then give the gift of time to your salespeople—time to actually *sell*.

Attendee SRDs

- Do you have something you want more information on or feel unclear about? Then ask to have it covered at your next sales meeting.

- Come prepared to learn from others' successes—how they met certain challenges and what they did to overcome them. Ask questions. Don't sit back and sulk in sorrow at your lack of pipeline activity.

- You know what to expect here, don't you? Come prepared with your answers to these questions: What's the movement on your prospects? What's brand-new in the pipeline? What's closing this week? Preparing your answers will make your life a whole lot easier. (Warning: If those answers never change, then your life will be less burdened with sales meetings. Instead, you'll be home on the couch with no job.)

Use sales meetings as an opportunity to praise performance, provide up-to-date instruction, and deliver resources to develop top-shelf sales behaviors and attitudes. Unplanned sales team meetings lead to unmotivated sales team members, the same boring results, and the same level of growth.

Get Out!

Take a moment to schedule a client meeting during your regular sales team meeting. But if you don't come back with some measurable results after doing this a few times, your boss will quickly catch on.

Online or Virtual Meetings Suck

Warning: What's *exponentially* worse than a meeting that sucks? An online or virtual meeting that sucks!

In the words of Shakespeare, "A rose by any other name smells just as sweet." Well, no matter what you call Webinars, online conferences, or virtual meetings— whatever name you come up with for meetings via computer connections—it still can smell stinky.

Go back to the technology discussion in Agenda Item 2, where I stressed that *you* are holding the meeting, not the technology. However, technology can either enhance or destroy your meeting. Webinars can be guilty as charged. They sound great on paper. A Webinar is any form of online meeting in which a presentation takes place in your office (or a host location) whereby attendees can converse, view, and interact via a shared workspace and broadband Internet connection. Attendees can be literally anywhere—in their office, in an airport, or even on their mobile device—yet they can see exactly what you are presenting in real time.

Virtual meetings potentially save you the hassle and cost of bringing everyone together physically, and as the concept of "office" expands globally, you have to do that, right?

Well, sort of.

The benefits are obvious. Meetings can now take place across remote locations on a moment's notice. This not only greatly reduces expenses but also expands your ability to collaborate audibly and visibly in real time. For control freaks, that means you're able to control exactly what everyone sees at the same time.

> **But—and this is a biggie—in a Webinar every presentation sin you have ever committed, every poor presentation skill you have groaned over, becomes accentuated *to the extreme*.**

It gets worse. Challenges and hindrances that weren't present in personal meetings now play into the equation of creating an effective meeting. I define these issues as *Six Degrees of Suckification*, because the meeting participants are separated.

These Six Degrees might cause you to think twice about how you proceed. They are, in no particular order:

1. Difficulty in reading the attitudes and knowledge levels of your meeting participants
2. Multitasking or disinterest by participants who don't engage in the content, thus your message fails to reach them
3. Connections, delays, lag time, or other technical difficulties causing physical communication breakdown
4. Poor presentation skills that are amplified to extremes in nonpersonal meetings
5. Misunderstood or misperceived communication from chat sessions or other text-only interactions
6. Prolific abuse of the "Overinvitation Syndrome" (and meeting frequency in general) because they're so easy and cost-effective to hold

While it's not my job to influence you for or against online meetings, let me say this: If you haven't participated in an online meeting yet, you soon will. Growth rates are sharply increasing for online meeting platforms and software providers, Webinars, and Web meetings of all types. Therefore, if you can't avoid them, how can you reduce the separation anxiety you face with your beloved conference table (yeah, right!) and minimize the Six Degrees of Suckification for online meetings? Consider the following SRDs.

Facilitator SRDs

- Don't think that smart meeting know-how doesn't apply because your meeting or presentation isn't face-to-face. In fact, rules about being prepared, concise, focused, and on point are even more important in this context. Participants' attention spans fall drastically if they're watching a digital screen and listening to a voice-over IP in place of interacting in person.

- Taking a show-and-tell approach sucks. Keep participants interacting and engaged by using polling, audio, text response, and other collaborative features. Use them, and use them often.

- Position a welcome graphic at the beginning of your Webinar so participants know they're in the right session. They might disconnect because they are distracted looking for the appropriate login code or password before the session starts. The welcome indicates that they are in the right Webinar.

- Turn off any instant messaging (IM) alerts and pop-ups if people are viewing your desktop for your presentation. No need for them to see that your significant other is missing you (when a message pops up on your screen). Also be aware of any desktop images, screen savers, or other open windows or file names that may be visible in a screen-sharing mode or when you flip back and forth between windows.

- Invite first-timers to your Webinar to join the session 10 minutes before the main meeting begins. During that time, review meeting etiquette, housekeeping

160

items, and proper use of the system. Or include a Web link in the invitation that provides them with basic instructions they should view ahead of time.

- If you're making a formal presentation internally to your team or externally to a prospective customer or client, rehearse it! Well! Your speech flow, tempo, and inflection are all key factors in maintaining an engaged audience, *even more so than in person*. You don't want to fumble with the software or even your tone of voice.

- If you know that participants might need a specific plug-in for their Web browser, include the link where they can download and install it before your online meeting begins. If you don't do this, you have just guaranteed yourself a 10-minute-late start.

- Use the record feature available on most conferencing systems for documentation or for those who are unable to attend. But be cautious if your meeting contains confidential information. Don't allow it to be e-mailed around. Keep it on a secured location with assistance from your IT department.

- The larger your online group becomes, the more you may want to consider a controlled question-and-answer or collaborative format. You need to control who has access to the drawing tool, chat box, or mouse. If you don't, mouse-control envy will set in and lead to the demise of your meeting; it's just too tempting for attendees to reach for control.

Attendee SRDs

- All meeting preparation rules for attendees still apply, as do opportunities to keep the meeting on track. Just because you can hide behind your monitor doesn't mean you should hinder the potential of achieving more robust results or get other things done when you can be an active participant in this meeting.

- Strive to interact when appropriate. Your collaboration stimulates others to interact, thus keeping everyone involved.

- If you're new to online meetings, then do some homework to understand how best to use it. Don't slow down the meeting's progress because of your lack of system knowledge.

- No matter how hard you try to flip ahead to the next pages and get to whatever is coming up, it's just no use. The facilitator controls the slides!

- Always set your webcam to manually enable if you're using one. At the same time, be aware of the setting in the software platforms that could automatically enable your webcam. *Wow*, so many ways this could possibly go awry . . . none of them good.

- Throwing stress balls at the monitor will have no actual effect on the meeting. But if it's your first time, a stress ball pitch might actually reduce your anxiety about the Webinar or online meeting.

Get Out!

Connection drops or other issues can prevail and make for a perfectly realistic reason to avoid responding to a question asked—or being "present" at all. But you'd better be prepared to record the meeting so you can watch the session later to glean the relevant content. The bonus? You get to play back the hour-long meeting in half the time and save 30 minutes of your day.

You could also outsource your attendance to a third party. That person can "raise your hand" for you when the facilitator confirms that all are still paying attention. Then you're free to finish the report you're working on.

Videoconferencing Sucks

In 1994, my first *real* job was as an inside sales rep for a start-up desktop videoconferencing (DVC) company in Washington, D.C. Previous to that, for my senior term paper at Ohio University in Athens, Ohio, I wrote "End User Support for Videoconferencing." I also worked in the telecommunications department as a student managing the videoconferencing units while I attended university. Based on this, I'm proud to say I have considerable insight, experience, and historical knowledge about why videoconferencing sucks. (Well, back then it really sucked, but it sure seemed cool at the time.) It wasn't that the technology didn't work; it sucked because meeting participants let the technology take over. They thought the technology would somehow magically create an unforgettable experience.

That was then, and this is now. Dare I say, vast and exponential leaps have been made in the technology? People have become more accustomed to its use, and it's even readily available for free via Skype, Yahoo!, AOL, and other online media. In addition, high-definition telepresence videoconferencing has emerged. These provide a high quality of video and audio that have made this way of conducting meetings a power to be reckoned with.

Yes, videoconferencing has its bennies. It eliminates expensive travel time because physical location doesn't

163

matter as long as reliable bandwidth and adequate equipment are available.

Know what's really cool? Ad hoc meetings across continents now happen in a virtual face-to-face format. Nonverbal communication in the form of body language reenters the meeting environment, which can greatly enhance engagement, interactivity, and the overall ability to communicate. Go team.

The Six Degrees of Suckification apply here. And I'll add one more. None of the benefits implies that effective use of this technology can be obtained instantly. Also, you face issues that are specific to this meeting type— from potential complicated technical issues to the type of clothing that works best on the television or computer monitors.

My pet peeve with videoconferencing is that it's too easy for people to talk over one another. Not everyone has a powerful enough computer to run videoconferencing effectively, so potential delays in conversation (communication lags) can add more frustration than productivity. You also deal with the shorter attention spans inherent in using technology, so strict adherence to agenda and increased levels of preparation should be the norm.

If you're new to videoconferencing or concerned about how to act or even what to wear, here are a few SRDs you can apply right away.

Facilitator SRDs
- Keep up energy and interaction levels, which is important because of the increased difficulty of maintaining participants' attention.

- Have an experienced technician on-site when using complicated systems.

- Unless this is a one-way broadcast presentation (i.e., no feedback from the audience), your ability to keep the number of attendees to a minimum will enhance your ability to get things done.

- Realize that due to more one-way communication, possible lags or delays, and the absence of some nonverbal communication, videoconferencing takes more time than a comparable in-person meeting.

- Learn to control the camera and remote control well in advance, if that's your responsibility.

- Get the timing right. A never-ending meeting can be highly costly if you're working in rented space or paying for the equipment by the minute.

- Address people by name every time. While you may be looking at them on the monitor, it may not appear so from their seat.

- If you use a webcam, carefully and intentionally compose the background that participants will see. Avoid bright lights behind you, clean your desk, and look for glare from picture frames or artwork.

Attendee SRDs

- Establish eye contact by looking into the camera instead of looking at the screen.

- Cameras can read lips. Think you're not on? Guess again. In an in-person meeting, you know when someone isn't looking at you. In video mode, you don't.

- Avoid doing something in the background that is highly personal; don't eat or drink while the meeting is in progress.

- Curb your urge to immediately check your phone each time it buzzes with new mail.

- Be prompt so the meeting can start on time. Time is money in every sense of the word.

- Speak in a normal tone of voice. Even though other participants are a long way away, they can still hear you. Don't be annoying by talking louder and slower.

- Don't wear loud clothes. Bright-colored, busy-patterned clothing can affect the video quality on lower-grade systems. Wearing natural or muted colors tends to work best. All-light or all-dark colors can create contrast or white-balance issues and make your skin look weird on camera.

- Brush your teeth. While others can't smell your bad breath through the screen, they *can* see that spinach piece in your teeth.

- If video-based meetings are the norm for your business, then keep that shirt, sweater, blouse, or tie handy at a minute's notice for impromptu meetings. Don't worry; your boss won't be able to see your shorts and golf shoes.

Oh, and one more thing. While amazing full-room HD systems are available (and incredibly cool and reliable), even the free desktop systems are impressive and simple to use. But remember, it's still a meeting, and unless you want your 15 minutes of fame to bore, all the rules apply.

Friday Meetings Suck

Um . . . enough said? Hope you get the point.

Facilitator SRDs

- Unless this meeting concludes at a local watering hole, let this team finish the week on the projects, sales, or tasks that *need* to be completed this week. Then, instead of going home with a load of anxiety and stress, you can leave work with a sense of accomplishment, which you feel most acutely on a Friday (or worse yet, Monday) for all the things that didn't get finished because you'd called a Friday meeting.

Attendee SRDs

- When you get the invitation, suggest a new time that would fit better.

Get Out!

Funny how it seems your calendar is always *completely filled* with other things on Fridays. That's a good habit to keep up! Schedule yourself for personal work time so your calendar shows up as full and others can't "automatically" schedule your time.

Have a productive Friday, and a great weekend!

Agenda Item 7

Big Meetings Suck Even Bigger . . . Get Some Help or Suffer the Consequences

No single activity in business is more impactful upon subordinates than holding a meeting that is engaging while being specifically targeted toward a company objective. No other activity in business can allow the C-Level executive to deliver a message, while following through with the social interaction so critical to today's workforce.
—Chris Curry, CEO, Destinations by Design, professional event management

For the most part, this book is about everyday office meetings and all the myriad ways they can go bad. With the fast-paced, complex nature of our times, we may well have a need for *more* meetings to share information, build consensus, and so on. Meetings help pull team members together to align with a single vision about how and why they'll succeed in their organizational endeavors.

Yet I'm not talking about your everyday office meeting in this section. It's about the large meetings that seek to bring the masses together and might include attendees from both within the organization and outside of it. These "big" meetings can be highly successful, and they are also

169

highly visible to your boss and other executives. But because of their size, everything that sucks about a regular old meeting becomes amplified here. Even more than a project meeting get-together, the Big Meeting can quickly engulf time that should be spent doing your "real" job.

That holds true for those attending as well as those planning this type of meeting. If you're the lucky duck who gets to plan one of these, you will be taken deep into territory that could be quite unfamiliar to you—the world of contracts, logistics, caterers, and event planners.

If you're an attendee, you don't get to just sit back and enjoy the show. You still have some responsibility for making the meeting go well. So read on. You never know when you're going to be asked to step up and help plan one of these monsters, and somewhere in the back of your mind, you may remember that a book you read about "boring meetings" had something useful to say about the whole deal.

Poorly Planned Meetings Suck

So, you want to have a Big Meeting or have been asked to plan one, huh? You've always wanted to have the opportunity to be that bright, shining star who gets pats on the back and "you-were-the-hero-of-the-event" comments from your boss or CEO. You may be tempted to pass the buck to another committee head or avoid the project altogether, but that tease for your time in the spotlight has great appeal.

Where do you begin?
What questions do you ask before starting?
How do you sell the whole deal to your boss and ask for a substantial budget?
Whom do you work with?

If you're looking for quick SRDs on typical Big Meeting types, don't worry they're coming. But if you want to look like the shining star at your event, then heed the following advice on managing meetings strategically. Or else? Or else your big meeting might just suck even bigger!

One of the greatest meetings-industry challenges is confusion about how to achieve real value with meetings and events, especially in our postrecession economy. This has led to a reduction in certain facets of meetings that don't have a clear set of goals and a path to accomplish them.

Yet meetings are a fact of life, so why not ensure that face-to-face meetings on grand scales continue to take place? They need to thrive with a strategic design that provides a return on investment for all stakeholders and attendees. We not only need to effectively manage big meetings, conferences, and conventions, but make a clear business case for this return.

> *We have an unprecedented opportunity for truly strategic discussions between the people who plan meetings and the senior executives of public and private organizations that sponsor them. Now, more than ever, the topic of meetings and events has great relevance in the eyes of powerful stakeholders.*
> —Mary Boone, President, Boone Associates

For some organizations, gone are the days of, "Here's $2 million; let's have a company meeting." Yet the companies that realize that this same $2 million can deliver an increased focus and commitment on strategy, mission, and objectives can excel in massive ways.

Wait, you don't have $2 million? Not even 20 grand? It doesn't matter if you're the executive assistant who's been "voted in" or the association executive who's planning that team meeting, annual membership event, or company off-site extravaganza. The same basic concept applies.

Whether you have 10 or 10,000 attendees, take a few minutes to understand how to have meetings that have meaning and value instead of a room filled with disengaged people. Then you can make your large event *rock* instead of *suck*!

Managing Meetings Strategically

Instead of providing more SRDs here, I'll let someone else do the talking—for once. Mary Boone, is a meetings industry author and authority on organizational communication, leadership development, and large-scale interactive meetings. In her "Four Elements of Strategic Value," Mary Boone shares four issues to consider when designing strategic meetings:

1. PORTFOLIO MANAGEMENT
In the portfolio of all the meetings for your organization, how does this event align with the organization's overall goals and objectives compared with others? The more precisely in tune with the fundamental mission, the more of an investment it's worth.

2. MEETING DESIGN
Meeting design is the purposeful shaping of the form and content of a meeting to achieve desired results. Here you decide how to address the form and human interaction of the event. This means incorporating the methods and even technology that inform, connect, and engage your group before, during, and after the meeting. Solid meeting design helps the meeting owner establish clear objectives and desired outcomes. Based

on this meeting design and goals, the meeting planners (internal or hired) would then execute the details and logistics of the event.

3. Measure the Impact
Meetings should be measured to better understand how the attendees see the meeting: Is it relevant, important, useful, challenging, and motivating? You can measure how much your attendees learned by their ability to capture the actual takeaways of gaining new information, feeling more connected to the information and team, making new contacts, or developing new skills.

4. Logistics
The meeting logistics are separate from the form and content of the meeting. The logistics are the physical execution of the design plan and its desired results. How are you going to accomplish this efficiently and effectively?

While any professional planner can detail for you how the size and shape of a room, temperature, the quality of the sound and video systems, the ability of attendees to interact and move about, as well as basic table layout can dramatically impact what can be accomplished at your event, they need a strategic design to work from to accomplish organizational return on investment.

If setting all this in motion has you feeling overwhelmed, don't be. Take the time to investigate working with a professional event planner who understands strategic design and can assist with your effort to develop one for your next large meeting. If you are looking for help, reference professional industry groups
(continued)

Big Meetings Suck Even Bigger . . .

(continued)

that have seasoned experts, not a bunch of fly-by-night people who just plan parties. These include Meeting Professionals International (www.MPIweb.org), the International Society of Special Events (www.ISES.com), the National Association of Catering Executives (www .NACE.net), and the Professional Convention Management Association (www.PCMA.org). The local convention and visitors bureau in your event city can direct you to reputable suppliers.

Make no mistake, there's a *big* difference in meeting planner folks. As a keynote speaker, master of ceremony, and creative director for large and small events, I've worked with dozens of event planners. Some get it and some don't. Find the ones who take the initiative to educate themselves and strive to improve the meaning in your meetings, not simply someone who helps you "plan a party." These are generally the professional planners who take the time to continue their education and expertise to the benefit of the clients and clients' budgets. (Note: You may even notice the Certified Meeting Planner (CMP) designation from Meetings Professional International. This is an advanced degree within our meetings-industry world that encompasses a great deal of work, effort, and knowledge.)

Don't Fall for These Meeting Planner Myths

But wait. You don't think you can work with a professional planner? Worried that you could lose your job? If you feel overwhelmed by the responsibilities and under the gun to pull it all off in far too little time, keep the following meeting planner myths in mind when you search for a good meeting planner.

1. *"Hiring a meeting planner will cost more than doing it myself."* While it's difficult to say you'll save money with a planner (too many variables at play), a planner will often allocate efficiencies that ensure budget money is spent on items that truly matter to the meeting's objectives. They will also help with efficient use of food and beverage budgets and good planners can even improve on corporate hotel rates. They may have national contracts that ensure better rates than a local hotel sales office can offer. This alone can equate to huge savings in lodging, food and beverage services, transportation, and audio-visual production.

2. *"Meeting planners would just do the same thing I would do."* In some cases, they might, but what's your time worth? Plus, look at the experience and expertise factors. Seasoned planners can navigate minefields for you. Chances are they've had things blow up before and now know what to do. Why not take advantage of those lessons learned? And why not let the meeting planner check on breakfast being ready at 6:00 AM instead of you? Your executives will feel well cared for and appreciate that you coordinated this seamless event.

3. *"But we've done this annual meeting for five years with the same format and everything has gone great. Why change now?"* This could be the very reason you need to bring some new ideas into your event. Meeting planners know what works; they can help design strategic concepts that deliver a *measurable* ROI. Maybe this will lead to increasing the budget so you can plan that event you've always wanted to have. Whether your meeting is for education, networking, or celebration, a planner is an invaluable resource who brings a myriad of fresh, creative ideas.

175

But enough of the commercial. If you're planning a big meeting—heck, even if it's on the small side—get some professional help. Your attendees will love you, which means your boss will be happier, which means . . . get the picture?

Annual Meetings, Conventions, Teambuilding, and Company Retreats Suck

These are the Big Ones of the Big Meetings. They comprise about 99 percent of all the Big Meetings held. And you know what? I'm not suggesting that you cancel them. No way. They have the potential to be too valuable—to tap into that "intellectual" and "social" capital Chris Curry talked about in the quote at the beginning of this section. They are just too darn important.

In truth, this chapter could really be titled *"Poorly Planned* Big Meetings Suck." The Big Ones aren't bad in and of themselves, but lack of planning and *knowledge of what to plan* makes them suck.

Generally, the root problem of these types of meetings (and this is true for all) stems from this: Those who plan 'em don't have a strategic plan for the event's value and return on investment, and they don't know how it falls within the grand scope of the overall organization's mission. Once this return on investment is determined, it needs to be communicated to the masses.

Here are three typical responses to an invitation to the company retreat:

1. "Awesome. Let's party!"
2. "I think this will be good. We've been putting in a lot of hours lately and could use a stress reliever and

some fun motivation. Plus, we need to get the whole organization in tune and focused on what it is we're really doing here."

3. "Oh great . . . not only do I have to work with these people, now they are making me play with them! Singing 'Kumbaya' by the fire together doesn't really help me get this report finished."

Which response would you prefer?

I posted a question to my social network asking people about their thoughts on the annual company meeting and here were some of the less than flavorful comments.

The annual company meeting is:

- Where you are reminded of how many different levels are between you and the CEO.

- Where you have no personal input.

- Where you see the big rollout of the new products that you don't hear anything about after the meeting except for the big colorful posters in your break room that detail the trip to Vanuatu you know you won't be going on.

- Where you have to remember those people's names in accounting.

- Where you come face-to-face with Mischievous Michael, who is always causing trouble for you, and now you have to have dinner with him.

- Where you learn everything you've been doing is wrong, and there's a new way you should be doing it.

177

- Where the corporate offices tell you about what's happening in *your* region and how your business unit will be run, even though they've never been there.

- Where you wish they hadn't spent $25,000 on that band and instead had fixed the copy machine.

Don't get me wrong. There were just as many positive comments as well, ranging from having opportunities to network, learning from the best, engaging in new learning or selling techniques, and personal motivation and team cohesion. You can read into them however you like. *In general on the negative side, though, attendees felt as if they were being preached to instead of being a part of the solution.*

Why do we spend so much time at these big meetings preaching about the content and so little time reinforcing the successful behaviors that got us here—or those that need to be in place to get us where we want to go?

Did you know that in almost any given profession, your ability to get that job done effectively while dealing with constant change is 80 percent based on your behavior and only 20 percent based on your knowledge? Why don't you go back to your notes and take each speaker from the conference and separate the material they presented into "content" and "behavior" buckets and see which fills up first.

"Attitude Is Everything" isn't just a fancy poster on the wall, after all.

While once again the opportunity presents itself for an entire book on this one topic, here are just a few things to consider that may help you plan a big meeting.

178

Organizer SRDs

- Communication goes both ways at these events. If you communicate to your audience but do not request any feedback, they can feel isolated. Also, spewing content or facts and figures at them all day will lose its effectiveness quickly.

- Which activities, speakers, or trainers would be best received for the entire organization or individual groups?

- Would everyone be physically and emotionally comfortable on the "ropes" course or playing softball? How will others view attendees if they are not successful at this activity? What activity option can I offer these people?

- What do I want attendees to remember once they've returned to their offices? What habits do I want them to change?

- Failing to communicate with all key players and outside speakers on the key messaging points and company initiatives can result in inconsistent experiences.

- Attendees should know why they are attending. What are the expected outcomes after the event?

- Wearing jeans and a flannel shirt doesn't spell creativity. If this is your creative idea to have people interact differently, you're in trouble.

Unless you have structure and goals for your meeting, then it's just a fun day off for many attendees. If you hope to ignite this team to greater productivity, cohesion, and focus, then you must realize the need for planning. Just being at an off-site location, smearing mud on your faces, and roasting marshmallows over the fire will not cause these things to happen, so please don't fool yourself or your attendees. You'll come back with great stories, yes, but once they're back in the office, most everyday routines and habits instantly set back in.

Bad Audio Sucks

A meeting you can't hear isn't a meeting!

Tap, tap, tap. . . . *"Is this thing on?"* When you're at the lectern, saying this is nearly as bad as the gut-wrenching, horrific sound of that silver bendy thing that holds the microphone at the lectern when you try to adjust it for another person.

Did you know that microphone feedback scores higher in terms of being an irritating sound than fingernails on a chalkboard? This was based on a study by the Acoustics and Audio Engineering Department at the University of Salford in the United Kingdom. (The sound of someone vomiting came in at number one. Coincidentally, that's what I feel like doing when I show up at an event where the audio sucks.)

A meeting that can't be seen can still be a meeting if the information is conveyed audibly. An effective conference call is an example. However, if your message breaks up or in any way, shape, or form and the attendees can't *hear* it, it's time to quit.

What also sucks is a speaker who is uncomfortable with a microphone, or who doesn't know how to use one, especially when microphones are readily available. Once, I was a featured entertainer at an awards banquet with about 500 attendees. The banquet hall had a stage, a lectern, a high-quality audio system, and stage lights, to boot. Audio was set up for my show as well as the DJ following the show, with multiple microphones at the ready.

The vice president of sales strode onto the stage along with the operations manager to begin the awards and talk about their teams. The VP began to speak and was barely audible in the back. Nearly right away, you heard the stereotypical "Can't hear you" yell from the back, and the DJ hurried to the stage to offer one of his microphones and the option of the lectern, which was equipped with a microphone.

Did that VP take it? No—he pushed it away! "I'll just talk loud!" he said.

Now we have the big boss, arms flying about with excitement and nearly completely inaudible by two-thirds of the audience. I was sitting in the back row, which was full. I looked around and saw people messaging, talking among themselves, making phone calls, and doing everything *but* attempting to listen to their boss. They simply gave up. This organization undoubtedly spent a great deal of money to fly these people all together, feed them, and give prizes to their winners. The end result? *Zero* on a scale of effectiveness. The winners still received their gift certificates, but their peers in attendance had no idea what they had won or even why. It was a miserable failure, and the award winners received no actual recognition.

How about those people who take the microphone and hold it at their waist? Or those who gesture with the hand that's holding the microphone, such that their dialogue goes in . . . and out . . . and in . . . and out again. Yeah. Good luck.

John Page, the principal at Pagetech Limited, a premier audio and visual production company, suggests that you

181

hold the microphone like a rock star does. At most, hold it just a few inches from your face. Don't be afraid to make some noise and fill the room with audio, as a qualified audio tech will always adjust the amplification or tweak it as needed. When you hold it at your waistline, the tech can only turn it up so much. Also, know that if you can't hear yourself through the PA system, then no one else can, either.

Organizer SRDs

- An empty room sounds different than a room with 20 or 200 people in it. People act as sound dampeners. If you are not working with an audio professional on-site, listen to the level in each corner of the room until it sounds clear in all areas. Then, tweak it up a notch. It will sound slightly uncomfortable at the time, but you'll be thankful later.

- Ask the venue or audio technician how to control the sound. Know which dial controls the music and each separate microphone. If they're not marked, mark them. It's a good idea to know how to run the basic soundboard. Ask the technician at your next event for some pointers. Most (but not all) are happy to help.

- If *you* are the meeting planner, request a high-quality audio package from the meeting center, or hire an audiovisual company. *Yes*, it *will* cost you money. Either spend the money on good audio or waste your money on the entire event. You pick! Better to spend $500 and have a successful meeting then to spend $30,000 (as the company in the preceding example did) and suck the wasted money down the drain.

Speaker SRDs

- If you're speaking at a meeting of larger size, arrive early and test the room. Your meeting organizer should have planned ahead of time for the amplification you will need. The people in the back row need to be able to hear you loud and clear, as well as any "quiet talkers" you may have. If they can't, thanks for playing, but your guests aren't staying.

- If the microphone makes you nervous, you must get there ahead of time and practice. Practice *not* fidgeting with the cable, tapping the lectern (which also amplifies), or pausing in very large venues (the delay factor can sometimes throw you off).

- Hold the microphone to your mouth, not your gut. The audience is interested in what you're saying, not what you had for lunch. Or ask for a lapel microphone and tune that in appropriately during your sound check. (Did you notice? I said sound check . . . as in *preparation.*)

- When you walk up to the lectern, adjust the microphone to your face, if needed. God forbid you are using one that has the silver bendy thing that wreaks havoc when you move it, but if you do, bend it quickly and don't keep adjusting it.

- If you simply don't have access to the microphone, leave the stage and work the audience. Keep yourself moving and interacting with the different sections of the audience. Hearing 50 percent of your presentation well and 50 percent not very well is far better than not hearing it at all.

Attendee SRDs

- If you're in the back and can't hear, stand up, walk to the front, and stay standing up. Make the nonverbal motion of "No one can hear you." If you don't, who will? Otherwise, all is lost for those trapped souls in

183

row 44-B. (See, I told you that you would have some responsibility in this!)

From a professional speaker's standpoint, always use a microphone. *Always.* Even for a room of 30 people. It's not only courteous for those in your audience, it's essential for keeping them engaged and keeping *you* the center of attention and in command of your performance. If your voice merely provides background noise or is mildly audible, even the strongest of messages, stories, or content can be lost—guaranteed.

And please, please, please *stop* doing the *tap, tap* . . . *"Is this thing on? Can you hear me?"*

Distractions Suck

It's inevitable that someone's phone will suddenly and unexpectedly begin that obnoxious or symphonic ring tone we've come to love. Ever hear that? When it happens, everyone surrounding the guilty party can't help but mentally sing along and finish the next few bars of the song in their own heads. The owner scrambles to silence it, looking perplexed about who could be calling right now. More perplexing to me are those people who decide to go ahead and answer it and actually have a conversation, which is rude to the speaker and everyone else present.

Still, the ever-persistent *distraction* occurs. Electronic devices are ubiquitous, and most people know they should silence them. But don't expect people to turn them all the way off. As previously mentioned, I expect people to have them on. They may be using them for information gathering from people not in the room, for tweeting about the room temperature to the meeting planner, or to disseminate information immediately to people back in the

184

corporate office who couldn't attend, so let's leave that one behind. Now, what about the door that makes the loud noise *clank-click* with each entrance and departure? All of us just *have* to know who came in or bailed out, and we glance in the direction of the exit. Attention is lost, and the presenter has to work doubly hard to get it back.

As a professional entertainer, I know that timing in comedy or magic during a presentation is based on finding the perfect moment to focus attention, reveal the punch line, or deliver the visual gag. As a professional entertainer, I know my perfectly timed comedic moment always seems to be exactly when that new employee, Junkyard Jeremy, just happens to drop the full tray of dishes in the kitchen. The result? Both Jeremy and I look like bumbling fools.

In large or small meetings, sudden or continuing distractions cause your meeting to go from *showtime* to *sucktime* in one second flat.

A personal favorite: I'm speaking to a small group of about 75 people as the closing speaker for a company meeting. About 20 percent of the way into the program, we start hearing clanking of what sounds like glass. I then notice a multitude of beer bottles being passed throughout the audience . . . seriously.

My personal contract states that no food is to be served during a keynote, but I did neglect to mention beer. What was I to do as I was speaking about "creating impact" in who they are and what they do? *My* impact evaporated—quickly.

What did I do? Joined 'em!

Unprofessional? Yeah, no doubt. However, after toasting, we laughed, had a few words, and then they all immediately reengaged. I added more comedy than content and made it a great presentation.

> **Sometimes, you just have to roll with the punches. If you want something to be perfect every time, don't choose live events as your career specialty.**

What haven't you thought about that might act as distractions at your meetings? Consider these:

- Doors opening and closing. How many times might it happen in your meeting? How can you minimize it, or at least the distraction of it?

- Servers or waitstaff filling coffee cups or clearing tables. While they're sometimes courteous, tiptoeing around the tables, they can immediately lose that tact by loudly throwing a tray on the tray stand in the corner.

- Serving food or setting out food for the break in the back of the room.

- Hotel or conference staff cleaning the room next to you. Major clinging of stemware, with the vacuum to follow shortly.

- Staff pushing carts or joking with coworkers in the "private" employee-only corridors (the walls are so thin, everyone can hear their banter).

- Batteries going out in the microphone of the speaker. (See "Bad Audio Sucks.")

- People who depart to the hall to take that all-important call—making that loud *clink-click* as they go— and speaking as if no one can hear them.

- The presenter's laptop's lapsing into sleep mode.

- Attendees getting hungry due to insufficient planned breaks or long-winded speakers.

- Room temperature issues. This varies based on humidity, number of people, and even time of day.

- Room setup and the attendees' position at the table in relation to the focal point of the meeting.

- Centerpieces interfering with the attendees' view and/or interaction with other people.

- Type of chairs in the room. Do you want people rocking back and forth?

- Markers for charts or whiteboards not working.

- Water jugs or other refreshments not being refilled during breaks.

- Need I mention bathroom treks, which relate to people walking through a meeting, plus the sound of the door as they exit and reenter?

- Then there's the meeting room that has wood floors. You can hear the solemn, echoing footsteps resonate throughout the hallowed hall on the long walk to the back door as someone makes a move to *get out*.

- Shall I continue?

What can you do about all these things? You can't avoid them—not a chance. Address them quickly and quietly in the large meeting environment to minimize the damage.

These ideas might prevent distractions from sucking your audience's "eyes and ears" to another place.

Organizer SRDs

- Keep the doors closed, but use gaffer's tape (a non-residue-leaving tape that most audio/video companies use for taping down cables and cords) to "open" the doors ahead of time. Push the handle and tape it down so the latch will remain in the open position. You can't stop people from going in and out, but you can stop that loud clanking noise. (Note: This may look ugly, but it keeps the doors much quieter.) Credit goes to fellow speaker Mike McKinley for teaching me this one.

- Unless absolutely unavoidable due to time constraints, don't allow the waitstaff to serve or clear during a presentation or critical portion of the meeting.

- Related to server or staff issues, you wish you could control them, right? Generally, the nicer the property or conference center, the more they understand the overall experience factor, but never leave that to chance. Clearly identify, communicate, and confirm your stance on when waitstaff can serve and clear. Your premeetings should address the exact time frame of those entrances and exits by all staff members. Set the ground rules with the crew captain.

- When possible, request to have some empty space between your meeting and other meetings taking place in the same hallway or venue. This will cut down on carryover noise.

- Always have a direct line of access to the service or catering captain.

- Keep centerpieces well below eye level.

- Opt for floors that aren't made of wood or other noisy materials.

Speaker SRDs

- Feeling gutsy? Here's one that Ron, a client from Nationwide Insurance, shared with me from the Insurance Accounting & Systems Association Convention: "I saw a presenter pull a ringing phone from his pocket, hold it up, and turn it off. He then put it into a padded mailing envelope and then into a box. He dropped the box on the floor and stomped on it several times before picking it up and throwing it in a trash can. He smiled at the audience and held up several more envelopes and boxes, all without saying a word. Not a single phone rang out loud during his entire presentation." Thanks for the idea, Ron. Good luck with that one, and let us know how it goes!

- Refrain from the line "Tell them I'm not here" when someone's phone rings. Just keep going, or if you're really gusty, actually go answer it yourself.

Attendee SRDs

- Stay put, but if you must move, do it during the transition between one speaker and another. Never move when the speaker is giving his or her main points unless you absolutely, positively *must* leave.

- If people around you answer a call during a presentation, hit them upside the head.

- If a speaker is presenting while food is being cleared, put your silverware on your plate *gently*, instead of allowing Clanking Clyde the server to do it.

- Don't sneeze during a presenter's punch line.

- In general, be courteous! Remember all those manners you learned (I hope) as a kid? Apply them here.

Guest Speakers Suck

Yes, I am a guest speaker at big meetings. Often. It's how I feed my wonderful family.

My mother read this heading and gasped, "You can't write that—people won't hire you anymore!" I love my mom—always looking out for her kid. But it's okay, I explained, because it's often true. Many guest speakers *do* suck, especially when they don't know the audience well or simply aren't a good fit. And their fees can suck the money out of the budget of those who hired them—when it could have been spent on a more qualified speaker.

Talented speakers, on the other hand, can alter behaviors, educate in ways that stick and motivate personal and professional habits. What if your speaker precipitated a 5 percent increase in productivity across your organization? What's it worth?

To hang out your sign to the world and call yourself a *speaker* is easy to do; you might have thought about doing it yourself. But, as a meeting planner, how can you tell a good speaker from a bad one? Doing a little homework can be a huge help. Paying attention to these basics will reduce the possible suckification you might face when working with guest speakers.

Organizer SRDs

- Know the primary purpose of your speaker. Is the meeting information-based, motivational-based, or entertainment-based? Will it be the kickoff to set the tone of the event, or will it be the wrap-up to tie everything together? Or are you looking for an after-lunch speaker with a great message about personal effectiveness to break up a day of industry speakers?

- Ability to engage the audience is the key. No matter what speakers present, if they bore your audience, they lose credibility and effectiveness, and your meeting will suck.

- Is the speaker a member of the National Speakers Association (www.NSAspeaker.org)? This association doesn't let just anybody join. Credentials and accolades are required before membership is granted. Professionals who belong to the National Speakers Association have at least been in the business for a while and have had some success. They didn't hang out an "open-for-business" sign last week.

- Find out what your speaker knows about your industry or working environment. The quicker and more effectively speakers can relate to audience members in their own language, the more effective they'll be in gaining their trust, attention, and desire to take action.

- Check their references and ask the following questions:

  ◦ How effective is this speaker in delivering a strong message?

  ◦ How skillfully does this person relate to attendees?

  ◦ Is the speaker able to work with the organization?

  ◦ What is this speaker's level of professionalism before, during, and after the event. (Does he or she act like a diva?)

- Realize that spending less money on a speaker than planned may save dollars in your budget, but if the

Big Meetings Suck Even Bigger . . .

connection to the audience is missing or your speaker doesn't hit the deliverables, you've wasted that money.

Speaker SRDs

- Take the time to know who's in your audience.

- Create an experience instead of merely meeting an expectation.

Guest speakers can be the most memorable component of any event. Take time to select wisely so that your speaker's contribution will be the best investment you make in the conference.

No Introduction and Bad Introductions Suck

"Heeeere's Johnny!"

For those in the know, you can even hear the music right now, can't you? Audience members cheer, the curtain opens slightly, and the star enters. He makes his way to center stage and swings that imaginary golf club—every night. People witnessed this classic introduction on nightly TV for the late, great "King of Late Night," Johnny Carson.

Let's assume that person being introduced is not a national celebrity or a common household name. All too often, the introduction goes like this: "Thanks, Pete. Nice work on your overview. We have a guest speaker with us today. He's next . . . and his name is, um, Jon Petz. And aah . . . here he is."

Audience response? Who the heck cares?!

This can happen even when the emcee has been given a written version of the speaker's introduction ahead of time! The emcee (or lack thereof) either lost it or chose the easy way out. The problem is compounded by you or your speaker not knowing how to fix it—and quickly.

Why is the absence of a strong introduction a problem? Because botched intros blemish the engagement factor of the audience. No credibility or reason for listening has been established. People in the audience are given no darn reason to tune in.

When it's well done, though, the introducer presells audience members on why they should listen to and believe the person who will next have the stage. The moment speakers spew out accolades about themselves and assert how smart and successful they are, listing all their awards and credentials, they risk being perceived as pompous jerks. Great way to start, huh?

What defines a *great* introduction? It's one that drives interest in the presentation itself, one that demonstrates the speaker's expertise in the subject matter, one that builds anticipation for what's about to be said, and one that promises listeners knowledge they can put into action.

What is it *not*? It is *not* reading a long bio of the speaker's life. Boring!!!

If we're talking about your boss, CEO, or someone everyone knows well, and you're all part of an internal group, that's a different story. You needn't say a lot. But what if you're bringing in your company's "big cheese" to speak at an industry association meeting and the audience has no idea who he or she is? You'd better have a solid introduction delivered by someone who can do it effectively. Otherwise, you'll look like a fool in front of your peers, and probably your boss as well.

193

Organizer SRDs

- Request the introduction ahead of time to avoid having the speaker jot something on a napkin 10 minutes before showtime. It looks unprofessional on both your parts.

- If it's printed in the convention program, do you really need to read an introduction? *Yes!*

- Preview the introductions of your speakers and request a shorter one if necessary. Or trim it down, if needed, using the same verbiage the speaker has provided. You may want to get permission from the speaker and share any suggested changes.

- If *you* are writing the introduction, stay focused on why the audience should consider this person someone they should listen to. What awards, titles, or industry and nationally recognized credentials does the person hold, and how does this relate to the audience? (See "Speaker SRDs" that follow.)

- If possible, listen to your introducer read the introduction beforehand. A poorly read or monotone introduction can hurt all the buildup you've put into this segment or keynote.

- Hire a professional master of ceremonies. Nope, they are not free, but it can be some of the best money spent in terms of engagement factors, effective transitions, and consistent flow of events. Call me! I can help.

Speaker SRDs

Consider these factors when writing your introduction.

- What do you want your audience to know about you that enhances your credibility? Talk in terms of accomplishments and recognition that directly relate to this audience and establish your expert status. Fill in the blanks here and you'll at least have a good start:

- Was instrumental in accomplishing . . .

- Best-selling author of . . .

- Grew revenue by . . .

- Exceeded quota by . . .

- Is an expert in . . . because . . .

- Add something personable to establish yourself as a real person and not some inflated ego walking across the stage.

- Prepare more than one version of your introduction. Have a longer one and a shorter one, an industry-specific one (if you're an expert in that industry), and one for a general audience that doesn't use industry-specific jargon or accolades. There may be very small differences here, but it can help people relate better once you hit center stage.

- Finally, send it to the host ahead of time. Then bring two printed copies to the program—one that you will again give to the host upon arrival and the second to give to the emcee immediately before the speakers go to the stage, because the one you already gave that person is sitting in a jacket pocket that is hanging over a chair at the dinner table (trust me on this one).

Bad Emcees Suck

All emcees—like all speakers—are not created equal. But all Big Meetings should have one or more. Why? Because the talented ones can elevate your event in multiple ways and make it memorable long after the last beer bottle has been passed in the back row.

Dealing with corporate and association audiences is never easy. They're typically sophisticated, jaded, and accustomed to "flash" in the form of high production values. As victims of a career's worth of long meetings, they quickly become bored. To up the energy level, the master of ceremonies has to be energetic, engaging, and entertaining, immediately and consistently. Otherwise, the engagement factor drops and so does the memorability of your event and reasons for being there.

This exact problem has become a sincere passion of mine, as I see, time and again, high-quality and attendee-focused meetings plagued with emcees who provide *suckiness* in the form of:

- Talking heads with no energy, emotion, or enthusiasm for what they are doing

- Uninspiring introductions and transitions from one segment or speaker to the next that lack interest and content

- Information inadequately delivered or presented at the wrong time

- Engagement practices that don't relate to the audience or to the overall objectives of the meeting

- Disengaged audience members who aren't connecting with the reason they are there

I believe the role of the master of ceremonies is not just to be a show coordinator who ensures an on-time event, but one that ensures the event attendees are fully engaged in the program, informed of what's

196

coming up, and reminded of the importance of what has taken place.

As an emcee, you interact with the audience and effectively transition speakers, honorees, media, and other functional elements of the show to maintain proper flow and emotional balance. You should understand how and when to use interaction, humor, emotion, music, and lighting elements to emphasize or minimize the impact of a message or objective. The emcee is *the* live-event personality whom attendees should relate to, laugh with, and trust for timely, accurate information when needed.

This is definitely a lot to ask for, especially if you can't control who it is. It could be the sponsor of the event, who literally paid for this stage time; your current association board president, who has no speaking skills; or Timid Timothy, who didn't show up to the planning meeting and thus was given the job.

Here are some easy things you can do to increase the impact of your emcee right away, whether you picked the person or not.

Organizer SRDs

- Identify housekeeping announcements and how and when they should be mentioned. These might be time schedules for the day, sponsor thank-yous, upcoming highlights, silent auction features, bus and hotel information, and other logistical information about the event as a whole.

- Provide written (in large type on separate cards) introductions for each speaker, and review them with your emcee.

- *Please* go over proper pronunciation of all names. Write them phonetically, as needed. I'm not Jon "Pettis" or "Peetz" and certainly not "Putz." It's pronounced Jon "Pets" (Petz).

- Ask your emcees to attend all rehearsals, including the sound checks. Have them become comfortable with the stage, and make sure they know where all talent, award winners, speakers, or executives will be entering and exiting.

- Help them understand the stage blocking and logistics you've planned for each element. No emcee wants to see anything get knocked over as the awards table is carried to center stage. Make sure your emcees know what's coming next.

- Be certain they have the proper microphone for their personal style. If they feel uncomfortable talking into a handheld device or tend to stray from the lectern, have them wear a lapel microphone or headset. If they say, "I will just hold it closer," realize that when they're in show mode, it won't happen. Don't leave this critical element to chance.

- Have backup scripts and introductions handy in case the original gets lost.

- Have visual or audible cues for delay, stretch, or hurry-up tactics and ensure your emcees know what they are.

Master of Ceremony SRDs

- As cool as you might feel, you're *not* the reason people have come to this meeting. Keep focused on why attendees are here and how you can enhance their experience. Set your ego aside and make the honorees or attendees the stars!

- Know your audience. Do your homework.

- Go over each name you'll be announcing. If you have any question about pronunciation, go find the person, planner, or client and nail it.

- Always comment about something that just happened onstage. For example, you might confirm any congratulations earned or repeat meaningful points made in the segment.

- Always have an appropriate 30-, 60-, or 120-second anecdote at the ready. Live events are *live* events; something unexpected always happens that might delay their momentum. Your story can fill in nicely.

- Never (please read that as *absolutely never*) have your material go "blue." Inappropriate jokes of a sexual, racial, or otherwise degrading nature should be absolutely avoided. Anything that even borders on PG-13 rating should be cleared with your organizer.

- Skills to become comfortable with:

  ○ Shaking hands. Seriously, you don't want to give or receive the dead-fish handshake on jumbotrons, I-Mag, or television.

  ○ Impromptu interviews onstage with award winners or executives. Remember that piece of homework? Get good at these interviews.

  ○ Microphones. Choose from handheld, wired lectern, lapel, or headset.

  ○ Confidence monitors. These are screens in front of the stage that prompt you about what's next, teleprompters, and in-ear prompters for larger events.

199

- ◦ Speech patterns. Go back and read about the *ums* and *aahs* in Agenda Item 5 for a refresher on what not to do.

A talented master of ceremonies can turn a great event into a *superb* event. Emcees accomplish this by delivering a consistent personality and tempo to the event while seamlessly tying the content and objectives together and keeping the audience engaged. When in doubt, hire a pro! As with hiring the right meeting planner, your ROI for hiring the right emcee is well worth the cash outlay.

Agenda Item 8

Heed This . . . or Continue to Suck for the Next Millennium

Have you ever really looked at the ROI on meetings? What are your meeting statistics? How many do you have a day? How much production gets done versus how many hours wasted? How much information do people retain once they leave a meeting?

I have written an entire book about how to make your meetings more productive, effective, and meaningful. I have teased, cajoled, and even threatened you to stand up and take responsibility for your meetings.

I could simply conclude this book with these statements: Meetings are about *you*. They are run by human beings and they are attended by human beings. Effective meetings can make the difference between an organization that simply survives and organization that thrives, and everyone is responsible for making a meeting successful.

But that quick summary would be boring.

Instead, I'm going to give you just a tad more advice . . . advice that I promised to give in Agenda Item 1 but, in true meeting fashion, have yet to deliver.

Remember our mantra? "Get In, Get It Done, and Get Out." Well, I hope you know by now how to get into your meetings more effectively and that you have even tried some of the new ways to get them done with speed and efficiency. But what about that "Get Out" part? I've provided some great tips in the form of SRDs in several places, but here's the full skinny on what you can do if you're stuck in a never-ending meeting, trapped by too many dogs off the leash, listening to presenter after presenter read from their PowerPoint presentations.

Consider Not Having One

My first piece of advice? When in doubt, *don't*. Who said you had to have a meeting in the first place?

I think many times we have meetings just to have meetings, because we want to appear busy to our peers, boss, and family, or because we simply don't know what else to do, and having meetings seems to be what everyone else is doing, so why not us?

There are a mass of things you could be doing instead of being trapped in the corporate closet of a conference room. However, there are certainly real reasons (and good reasons) to have face-to-face meetings. Determining the difference is the key.

Just to recap, a meeting is simply an assembly or conference of people coming together to achieve a common goal through communication and interaction.

Meetings may happen in person, via telephone, through videoconference, or in the form of online media interactive presentations. They can be one-time occasions (conferences), recurring (staff meetings with recurring objectives), or series meetings (recurring meetings with new objectives). No matter how you spin it, your normal meetings will fall into one or a combination of these categories:

- Planning
- Information sharing
- Evaluation
- Recognition

Typically, we default to a meeting when we need to address one of these group-collaboration categories. And the default result for many of them is, of course, everything this book is opposed to.

The first order of business should be to *exhaust all other options* to accomplish your objectives before scheduling time on people's calendars.

You and the others will greatly appreciate it, trust me.

Unfortunately, not being in your shoes, cubicle, swank office, or bathroom stall (thankfully), I can't tell you when to actually schedule a meeting versus retreating and posting the information to your local public or private information portal. But I can tell you this: Don't fall victim to the obsession of having a meeting when your solution, question, or challenge can be accomplished in another way.

> **Before you hit that Send button to speed your invitation on its way, *stop* and ask yourself:**

- How else can this information be shared, understood, or implemented without inviting everyone together? Does it have to be done face-to-face?

Heed This . . . or Continue to Suck

- Am I willing to do the necessary preparation to facilitate the meeting effectively and accomplish the objective?

- Who is a stakeholder in the discussion, what is the objective, and what is the desired outcome? Can I address it with this person directly?

- Am I hosting the meeting because I'm unsure in my decision?

- Am I calling a meeting just to make it look like my schedule is full?

If you answered yes to two or more of the preceding questions, then I strongly advise *against* having a meeting.

On the flip side, you could ask these questions:

- Will we reach a better-quality decision if we meet as a group?

- Will we be better committed to the solution if we meet as a group?

- Will the solution be better understood, implemented faster, and more effective if we meet as a group?

If you answered yes to any of these, then you should go ahead and press the Send button to distribute your invitation. However, before you have that meeting, make sure to review the appropriate sections of this book. Your test will be whether the participants actually leave feeling engaged and purposeful to the meeting, as it was a good use of time. If they do—you get a gold star! If they don't— you flunk. Go back and reread the appropriate sections of this book and try again. *Your* reputation is on the line, not mine, so the honor system stands firmly in place.

Good luck.

What you can do when a meeting sucks?

I'm going to fess up here. The stuff you just read is the nice stuff—the stuff that won't get you into any trouble and will allow you to "make nice" with your boss.

But now I'm going to let it all out. If you're in a meeting that sucks, and you have done everything I have told you to do, and you are truly are trapped, then read on. Please note: The author is not responsible for anyone partaking of said SRDs and getting fired. (Don't say I didn't warn you.)

What You Can Do When Stuck in a Boring Meeting

Let's face it, sometimes you get stuck attending a bad presentation, maybe for continuing education credit hours for your profession or because the political nature of your job or company requires you to be there. What happens then? You suck it up and smile.

But what happens *after* you have done the following?

- Cleaned out your in-box
- Texted your friends and family to finalize weekend plans
- Tweeted your whereabouts and frustrations
- Posted and commented on Facebook, LinkedIn, and any other darn social time wasters you have access to on your mobile device.

205

When all else fails, I hope the following attendee SRDs can add enlightenment and productivity to your minutes, hours, days, and years spent in boring and unproductive meetings.

Attendee SRDs

Here are some ideas for rescuing yourself from boring meetings or presentations.

Productive Activities

- Make or confirm your travel arrangements and check in for your flight home.

- Try one more excuse for why you should not be here.

- Do your routine work. Bring along files or documents you need to read or review. Refrain from typing unless others are taking notes.

- Start another meeting digitally. What can you accomplish with others in the room who also feel stuck? Get on your device and start a constructive dialogue with them.

- Have your favorite show downloaded on your phone, iPad, or laptop. If you have headphones, it's a good time to catch up. (Just one ear, though, as you lean your head on your hand.) Soon, many friends will want to join you on your pilgrimage so bring multiway headphone splitters.

- Make your to-do list for the remainder of the day and prioritize the activities.

- Calculate the "Snooze Factor." Count the total *zzzzzz's* of the meeting by adding together the *ums, aahs,* and *you-knows* uttered by the presenters.

Compare your score sheet with your peers to see which presenter scored the highest.

- Refresh the coffeepot. Take time to refill others' cups and offer them something to eat.

Fun Activities

- Try to get other people in the meeting to *crack up*. Send them a humorous text message. First one who gets caught laughing loses. Better keep them appropriate if you have a "principal" who may want to see what you're laughing about.

- Play "This Speaker Looks Like . . ." with your neighbor or with the whole group. For extra credit combine one of your neighbors and the presenter and draw a picture of their would-be children.

- Start the wave around the room when the speaker's back is turned. After you do this, post your video at www.BoringMeetingsSuck.com or on my Facebook page for a bonus prize.

- Play catch with a stress ball. How many catches can you make without getting caught?

- Play "Key Word." Confirm with others a key word that must be used in any questions or discussions and that doesn't relate to the topic. Example: Anyone who speaks must use the word *gymnasium* in their comment or question; first one who breaks stride loses! For extra credit, and to avoid getting caught in longer meetings, text new words to the players during the meetings. Bonus: It's a great creativity builder.

- Play "Bore-a-Gami." It's just like origami, and it's doable in a meeting. What can you make by folding one piece of paper? Have your peers all make the same thing as you and see whose origami is voted the best.

- Play "Buzzword Bingo" (or "BS Bingo," depending on your preference). Create a box chart with five across and five down, as in bingo. Fill each box with a typical buzzword from your office. Anytime a buzzword is muttered from the speaker, place an X in the box. If you get five down, across, or diagonally, then you win. Just make sure each player has words in different places on his or her chart.

  Need help with these buzzwords? These will get you started: maximize, out-of-the-box, benchmark, innovation, scalable, win-win, dialed-in, client, focus, action items, follow-up, economy, bigger picture, not rocket science, bandwidth, mobile, accountability, drill-down, leadership, repurpose, push the envelope, turnkey, that said, validate, and world class.

- Access games on your phone, iPad, or laptop from your friendly neighborhood app store. Here are some of my favorites:

  - Boring Meetings Suck (of course)

  - Meeting Sound FX

  - Fake Caller and Fake-A-Text, free and paid versions, which can be used in many environments

  - Games that can be played with other meeting participants via Bluetooth or WiFi are even better

- Play "Steal the Pen." Surreptitiously grab the pen from the people on either side of you. When you're asked if you've seen it, suggest borrowing one from the person sitting next to them. See if this chain of requests can make it all the way around the table. Note: If your neighbor has an extra pen and pulls it out, take that one, too.

- Play "Spin the Marker." Whoever the marker points to must answer or ask the next question, no matter what. For extra credit, combine this with the "Key Word" game for added excitement.

Absurd Activities

- Take photographs of the presenter using the flash and show them to other meeting attendees while the speaker is looking. Shout out loud, "See, I told you!"

- Bring an hourglass timer and set it prominently in the center of the table. Hold it up occasionally and look worried. Start gasping for breath when it gets close to the end.

- Play "Pass the Remote" by bringing a remote control from home and openly try to pause, fast-forward, mute or just plain stop this waste of time. Bonus points if multiple attendees bring a remote and all do it at once.

- Take bathroom or drink breaks, and each time you come back, be wearing something different. Better yet, have someone else come back and sit in your chair as though he or she has been the attendee all along. Switch again in another 30 minutes.

- Crawl under the table and unplug the presenter's laptop. At least the battery will eventually die.

Well, there you have it. How to have some fun, let off a little steam, maybe even prompt the meeting host, facilitator, or presenter to actually do a better job.

Heed This . . . or Continue to Suck

Conclusion

It is a fact. Boring meetings waste our time, energy, and talent, and they waste our employer's precious dollars.

We want to be productive in our workday. We want to show something positive for our work efforts. Meetings are there to help the work process along. A meeting is not an end in and of itself. Let's put meetings in their proper place! You don't have to sit back passively and take it. You can help the meeting flow more smoothly. You can help the facilitator get to and keep to the point when someone in the room is threatening to derail the meeting—or when the facilitator him- or herself is getting off track (or never found the right track in the first place).

Everyone who has to attend meetings in their work-a-day life must take charge. It is totally up to you. You can either sit back for the rest of your working life and just gripe and moan about how meetings waste your time, or you can do something about it. It is in your hands to change the world of meetings forever!

Have your team use this book. As previously mentioned, you don't need to read the whole thing. It's broken up into easy sections and chapters so you are able to jump right into what you need based on the meeting types you have. Keep it handy as a reference tool or supply it to every company library so the true Bore No More! movement can begin to take hold.

I wish you luck, and if you need any help—or more crazy advice on how to make meetings more bearable, and more memorable—don't hesitate to visit me at www .BoreNoMore.com. I'd also love to hear your best and worst meeting stories and tips for making them better at the book web site where you can also find other great information, technology updates and products to help your meetings be a Bore No More! All this can be found at: www .BoringMeetingsSuck.com

Now is your time! Are you ready?

Heed This . . . or Continue to Suck

Acknowledgments

Special thanks and appreciation to the Bore No More! and Boring Meetings Suck project team for all their hard work, dedication, and appreciation to eliminate meetings that suck: Dawn Ross, Sam Horn, Dr. Patricia Ross, Barbara McNichol, and Don The Idea Guy Snyder. Thanks also to the entire team at John Wiley & Sons Inc. for allowing me the opportunity to work with your prestigious organization and receive your support along the way. It was a pleasure to work with all of you on a project so important to me.

Thanks also to my loyal book supporters: Stacey Petz, Richard Petz, Bill Petz, Mary Coker, Sue Jacques, Bob Hothem, Chris Curry, Emily Chappie, Friday *wine* afternoons, and sitters Amanda, Emily, Larry, and Pat.

Additional thanks to the following contributors: Mark Henson, Brandon Dupler, Wendy Nicodemus, Amy Hiday, Rosemarie Rosetti, Randall Reeder, the Destinations By Design team for your hospitality and support, Deb Paat, Rebecca Garforth, Brad Copeland, John Page, Johnny DiLoretto, Diana Hisey, Kevin Gadd, Craig Morrison, Jim Samuel, Ron Borland, Tracey Tikos-Wiese, Becca Mount, Vanessa Mandell, Tony Tanner, David Corey, Ken Ritter, David Crone, Becky Nye, Colleen Gilger, Michelle Renda, April Manning, Jeff Williams, Mike McKinley, Frank

Pacetta, David Grady, Larry Hilsheimer, Cindy Hilsheimer, Kristi Penney, Bryan Suddith, Diana Carr, Jacee Scoular, Jack Windsor, Monica Filyaw, Martha Rose Sapp, Rob Eddy, Dave Ferree, Jill Clark, Dan and Lisa Clausing, Michael Kent, Randy Wilcox, Victor Paini, Greg Kelley-Flowers, Erin Gay, Tim Petz, Kari Osborne, Rob Barkley, Heather Didion, Garr Reynolds, Brenda Dyckes, Michael Dustman, Jodi Hoye, Jen Cassidy, Martha Mathews, Frank Addington, Chrissy See, Carrie Miller, David Cryer, Kevin Sloan, Terri Spring, John Armato, Stan Allan, Mindy Bailey, Seth Godin, Robb Martin, and all the others who posted, responded to, or otherwise contributed to ideas and SRDs that form the essence of *Boring Meetings Suck*.

(About the Author)

Jon Petz brings to *Boring Meetings Suck* his humorous perspective as a former corporate "warrior" once subjected to an eternity of boring meetings. He sat in a cubicle for years, made cold calls, dealt with corporate America, and grew in success to lead a national sales team with 52 offices. Today, he mixes this experience with his comedian/magician talents as Chief Engagement Officer of his own company, Bore No More!

This professional keynote speaker, master of ceremonies, and corporate magician has delivered presentations and performances worldwide for such prestigious organizations as IBM, JP Morgan, AT&T, Time Warner, and the U.S. government. All had him return in varying roles for multiple engagements. His contagious energy engages people with rich content and entertains them with a "twist" so they retain his message long after the meeting's end.

Jon is passionate about helping organizations get more out of their meetings—the reason he wrote this book! A master communicator, he clearly understands how to relate well to corporate planners, decision makers, and audience members alike. He energizes them to rekindle the passion in who they are and what they do. He also challenges them to create an impact beyond meeting expectations in their work, their lives, and the lives of others.

Jon, a firm believer in giving back, has been awarded the *CV Perry Advocate for Children Award* for founding "Miracles & Magic" with his wife, Stacey, in 2002. This Vegas-like comedy and magic show raises funds for children who have life-threatening illnesses—a program that continues to expand to cities across the United States. Also, in recognition of his professional accomplishments and community efforts, *American Business Journals* newspapers named Jon one of the top 40 business professionals under the age of 40 in 2008.

In addition to *Boring Meetings Suck*, Jon is coauthor of *Best of the Best* and creator of the DVD *Unlocking the Secrets*, both supporting his mission to help people Bore No More!

Jon resides with his family in Columbus, Ohio, where he enjoys working, performing, and coaching soccer. More about his professional and community contributions may be found at www.JonPetz.com; more about this book is located at www.BoringMeetingsSuck.com

Index

217

221

You have the book...now play the *game.*

The Mem-Cards go together perfectly with the book to reinforce productive meeting habits and can be taken right into your next meeting.

Use them to:

· Determine the best *Suckification Reduction Device* (SRD) for the meeting you are currently in

· Find new ways to get out of the meeting when needed

· Create fun things to do if you are trapped